The Best Fryer Cookbook Ever

Phyllis Kohn

A John Boswell Associates/King Hill Productions Book

HarperCollins*Publishers*

HarperCollins books may be purchased for educational, business, or sales promotional use. For information, please write: Special Markets Department, HarperCollins Publishers, Inc., 10 East 53rd Street, New York, NY 10022.

FIRST EDITION

Design: Barbara Cohen Aronica
Index: Maro Riofrancos

Library of Congress Cataloging-in-Publication Data

Kohn, Phyllis.
    The best fryer cookbook ever / Phyllis Kohn.—1st ed.
       p.   cm.
    ISBN 0-06-018764-6
    1. Deep frying.   2. Fryers, Deep fat.   I. Title.
TX689.K64   1997
641.7'7—dc21
                                               97-7174

02 HC 10 9 8 7 6 5 4

Acknowledgments

Special thanks to the deep fryer manufacturers who provided equipment to use in recipe development: Aroma Manufacturing Company, The Rival Company, DēLonghi America Incorporated, Krups North America Incorporated, Morphy Richards North America, and T-Fal Corporation. Gratitude also to Richard Braun of Zand & Associates, Deidra Cleary of PT & Company, Mark Schweiger of SHK Foods Incorporated, Wendy Burrell of The Burrell Group, Ltd., Martha S. Reynolds of Best Foods, and Susan Fuller of the California Artichoke Advisory Board for sending me products for use in testing, and to Susan Wyler for her continued support.

Additional gratitude to my tasters who so gallantly put aside their "fear of frying."

Contents

Introduction

Facts About Frying

Fried foods comprise a familiar and extremely popular part of our cuisine: succulent fried chicken; fisherman's platters piled high with golden brown fried shrimp, scallops, clams, oysters, and fish; and crispy fried appetizers—won tons, zucchini sticks, and breaded mozzarella cheese. What would a hamburger be without a side of crisp french fries? Or a cup of coffee without those sweet fried pastries we call doughnuts?

With a modern deep fryer, you can make all these dishes and many more in your own kitchen quickly, neatly, and with little fuss. Home cooking allows greater choice in choosing fresh, wholesome ingredients, recipes that are flavorful and reasonable in their preparation time, oils that are healthier, and a speed that keeps up with the tempo of our fast-paced lifestyle.

Success in deep-frying depends in large part on proper preparation of the food to be fried. This includes uniformity in size, both for appearance and for even frying. Fried foods need insulation, such as cornstarch or flour or a crumb or batter coating, to seal in flavor and keep the oil out. To help form a barrier, crumb-coated foods should stand at room temperature for 15 to 30 minutes to set the coating. If batter-dipped, enough batter must be used to coat the food completely. Too much absorbs too much oil; too little and the food is not protected. (Keep in mind that the richer the batter or dough, the greater the absorption of oil.)

Foods to be fried in the deep fryer should be at room temperature so they don't lower the temperature of the oil abruptly., Proper temperature is important, because fat absorption increases with the length of cooking time as well as with the amount of surface exposed to the fat. There must be enough oil to cover the food and to bubble up and circulate freely. In addition, ingredients should be added to the oil gradually, a piece at a time, and there should not be too much food in the fryer basket. At their best, fried foods turn out dry, crisp, and golden on the outside, tender and moist inside.

While no one advocates eating nothing but fried foods, some fat is necessary for good health. Just as a car needs oil and gas to keep all its parts working smoothly, our body needs fats in moderate amounts to function properly. Fats provide energy for daily activities, prolong digestion, and act as carriers for vitamins A, D, E, and K, which are needed for healthy skin and optimal growth.

But all fats and oils are not equal. Those with a high ratio of mono- and polyunsaturated fats to saturated fatty acids, such as olive oil, canola oil, and many of the vegetable oils—safflower, soybean, corn, peanut, sunflower, and blends of these—are considered better for your health. Others with a high saturated-fat content, such as lard, coconut oil, palm oil, and vegetable shortening, are thought to raise cholesterol levels. The most sensible plan is to choose wisely and eat a balanced diet.

Oils and fats enhance the flavors of food; that's what makes fried foods so irresistible. The choice of oil used is dependent upon the type of food being fried. More delicate, less highly seasoned dishes call for a neutral-tasting oil, such as corn, safflower, or a blend. For additional flavor, a stronger-flavored oil, such as olive or peanut, can be an enhancement. These oils are expensive but a better value if purchased in gallon-size containers. Chicken can be fried in a number of oils or solid fats. Many cooks swear by solid vegetable shortening; others use lard, which yields a very distinct taste and is often a must for fried chicken. For sweets, such as doughnuts, fritters, and fried pies, use a neutral-tasting oil, such as canola, safflower, vegetable oil, or a neutral blend. In many of the recipes in this book, I have left the choice of frying oil up to the cook.

For economy, oil can ideally be used 5 to 7 times. As the oil is reused, it will develop a deeper caramel color; this has no adverse effect. Just check to be sure that it has not turned dark brown, that it does not give off a strong, unpleasant odor, that it does not foam excessively, and that fried foods do not begin to taste of old oil. Oil for reuse should not be allowed to reach the smoking point.

The smoking point, which varies from oil to oil, is the temperature at which a fat breaks down into visible gaseous elements. If the oil begins to smoke, a sign of decomposition, turn off the heat immediately and pull out the plug. Let the oil cool completely for a minimum of two hours and then discard it in a proper manner.

Basically, there are two kinds of deep fryers. One is an open, multipurpose fryer, steamer, and slow cooker. The other appliance, dedicated to frying, is designed with a cover that contains a charcoal filter to eliminate odors and grease. Covered fryers are desirable because they prevent oxidation and decomposition of the oil during cooking.

The amount of food that can be cooked in a deep fryer is determined by the overall size of the model, its interior capacity, and the size of the fryer basket. Cost is determined by the number of special features, including the size and type of the machine, but generally prices range from about $30 at the low end to around $150 at the top; discount models are readily available.

When choosing a deep fryer, look for sturdy construction of the fryer basket and removable handles for ease of cleaning. Check out extra features, such as a viewing window, timer, cord storage, and nonstick feet. The majority of the models tested for this book are light in weight. All the covered models have a safety lock to latch the lid securely in place, and they are equipped with relatively easy-to-operate push buttons to open and close the fryer, an on/off switch, and an indicator light, letting you know when the oil reaches the proper frying temperature. Fryer baskets vary in design, size, and shape. All the covered models have minimum and maximum oil indicator marks located in the inside of the fryer tank. If the deep fryer does not have these indicators, fill the deep fryer no more than one-third full.

All the deep fryers have a temperature regulator that can be adjusted from 300° to 400°F. Some machines list these numbers; others note the frying temperature with pictures of popular fried foods or a "fry" range. If exact temperatures are not listed on your machine, be sure to use a deep-fry thermometer.

Cleanup with a deep fryer is simple. Fryer tanks have easy-to-clean interiors and exteriors. A few of the models boast removable fryer tanks, and the covered models have removable lids. This is a decided advantage when removing cooled oil from the appliance. One model features a rubber tube with a spigot at the end to siphon off the oil.

Once you have purchased your deep fryer, get comfortable with it before you start to cook. Read the manufacturer's instruction booklet; open and close the fryer; lift the basket up and down to get the feel of it; locate the minimum and maximum oil level marks. Be sure you know how to operate the thermostat control, and remove and replace the lid. The more you understand about how your deep fryer works, the easier it will be to deep-fry with foolproof success.

Like any cooking method, the most important consideration in frying is safety. Cooking oil begins to smoke only at extremely high temperatures. An accident is highly unlikely, since all electric fryers have heat settings that stop at 440°F., the temperature at which oil begins to break down. However, just in case, keep a heavy metal baking sheet nearby. If you see any flames when frying, immediately smother them with the baking sheet, turn off the thermostat, and pull the plug out of the wall. *NEVER* throw anything into the fat—water, baking soda, or sand. They will cause spattering and may increase the spread of the fire.

Safety First

1. Familiarize yourself with your deep fryer model before using it for the first time. Read all instructions that come with the machine; then *reread* them.

2. Attach the probe to the appliance first (on some models), then plug the cord into the wall outlet. To disconnect, turn to OFF, then remove the plug from the wall outlet. Finally, remove the probe from the appliance.

3. Place the oil in the fryer tank first, then connect the machine to the electrical supply.

4. Fill the deep fryer no more than one-third full or follow the manufacturer's minimum and maximum indicators located in the fryer tank.

5. Use the oils or vegetable fats specified for deep-frying. Do not mix solid and liquid fats together.

6. *Never* leave the fryer unattended or allow children to use the appliance.

7. Do not touch hot surfaces. Use hot pads or mitts for safety when touching handles or knobs.

8. The oil in the fryer will stay hot for some time after it is switched off. Do not move the fryer until it is completely cool.

9. Do not place the deep fryer on or near a stove, electric burner, heated oven, or under kitchen cabinets.

10. Do not use the appliance for other than intended household use.

11. Never lean over the fryer or place hands or face near the steam vent.

Deep Fryer Makes and Models

Several models of deep fryers and multipurpose cookers were used in the development of these recipes. The makes and models are listed in alphabetical order, which is not an indication of preference.

AROMA

Quik Fryer, Model ADF-135. A multipurpose fryer, steamer, and slow cooker that is definitely no-frills. Enamel model with enamel interior for easy cleanup. Illuminated on/off indicator light and carrying handles. Very small basket has removable handle that cannot be secured tightly. The thermostat does not include a temperature indicator, so you must use a deep-fry thermometer to be sure the oil is at the proper temperature. Temperature fluctuates about 25 degrees; recoup time—the time it takes for the oil to come back to temperature after frying the first batch of food—is relatively fast, about 5 minutes. Oil capacity: 6 to 8 cups. There is no timer or cord storage. Manufacturer's instruction booklet gives the necessary information for using the appliance and includes an 800 number. There are no recipes. Appliance has a 1-year limited warranty.

RIVAL

Chef's Pot, Model 23016. This basic black, nonstick, die-cast, 8-quart open kettle is a combination fryer, steamer, roaster, and slow cooker that is fully immersible in water. The appliance has a detachable temperature control, which adjusts to 400°F. The fryer basket comes with a clip that rests on the side of the kettle when lifted from the oil and which the company calls the "Drip-Grip." It works! Appliance stand on legs and has heatproof handles. Temperature control was off 25 degrees, which necessitates the use of a deep-fry thermometer. The recoup time for the oil to come back to temperature was relatively fast, about 5 minutes. Oil capacity: 7 to 8 cups. No timer. The manufacturer's instruction booklet gives information on how to use the model, but limited instructions on frying. Booklet contains a trouble-shooting guide and 6 recipes. There is a 1-year limited warranty.

DĒLONGHI

Cool Touch Roto Deep Fryer, Model D-20. This is 1 of the 2 most expensive models tested, but it has added features that other models do not. The slanted nonstick coated interior allows you to use half the amount of oil that similar-size models use, about 5 cups at the minimum level. Minimum and maximum oil-level markers in frying bowl were the most visible of all the deep fryers tested. Motorized fryer basket rotates at an angle, moving the food in and out of the hot fat. The fryer also has what the manufacturer calls an "exit oil system," located in front of the machine under a flip-out cover with a metal caution plate covering the plastic tubing. This drain tube and spigot make removing the oil quite easy, and the manufacturer supplies a long plastic pusher to insert through the interior of the fryer to eliminate any bits of food that might clog the opening of the tube. The appliance has a cool-touch insulated base and a seamless interior for easy cleaning. Push-button locking lid and lid opening button are easy to use. A viewing window in the lid allows you to monitor the frying process, but it tends to steam up, blocking the view. The lid can be removed with an easy snap-off clip, but cleaning the interior of the lid is difficult. There is a condensation evaporating system that allows steam to escape from the lid. The fryer basket was the largest of all the machines, but unless you hooked the handle just right when lifting and lowering the basket, it can fall into the oil. The machine also features a thermal safety device that automatically shuts off the unit should the oil overheat, a storage area for the cord, and a push-button 20-minute timer. The temperature adjusts from 300° to 375°F. The temperature fluctuates by as much as 25 degrees; recoup time for the oil was about 8 minutes. Oil capacity: 5 to 6 cups. The manufacturer's bilingual instruction booklet provides the most information on the use and care of the machine, including a picture guide to the machine and a troubleshooting list. Included is an authorized service center booklet with an 800 number. The manufacturer also supplies a package of filters to filter the oil after frying. There is a 1-year limited warranty.

KRUPS

Deep Fryer, Model 349. The largest of the deep fryers tested. Relatively light in weight, cool-touch exterior, and an easy-to-clean interior. Illuminated on/off switch, minute and second timer with an LCD display, and a loud bell tone telling you when the time is up. There is an anti-grease/anti-odor filter in the lid; steam escapes upward through the lid. The lid is removable, but it took me a long time to figure out how to remove it and then how to put it back on. The large-size, deep basket has a sturdy handle, which can be removed for cleaning, and is the most secure of all the baskets. The cord is contained in the base at the back of the model; it can be pulled out and pushed in when not in use, leaving just the plug exposed. Thermostat adjusts from 300° to 370°F. If you push the thermostat to the extreme right, the temperature of the oil will reach 375°F. However, the temperature did fluctuate by 25 degrees, and the recoup time is the longest of all the machines tested. There are minimum and maximum oil-level markers in the fryer tank. The touch-release button has a tendency to stick after repeated usage and I had to push it back into its normal position. Oil capacity: 11 to 12 cups. The instruction use-and-care booklet was clear and concise, but contained only 3 recipes. An authorized service center booklet was enclosed with an 800 customer service number. There is a 1-year warranty on the appliance.

MORPHY RICHARDS

Deep Fryer, Model 45102. A rectangular appliance with a removable, nonstick tank that is easy to clean. The fryer has a rectangular viewing window in the lid that the manufacturer tells you to lightly oil on the interior to prevent fogging up. The permanent filter is in the lid; the lid is removable and dishwasher-safe. The variable temperature settings range from 265° to 375°F., and there is an illuminated on/off temperature indicator, nonslip feet, and cord storage in the back. I thought the rise-and-fall basket was a wee too small for the size of the fryer. Minimum and maximum indicators are located in the tank, but were difficult to see. A condensation trap in the back of the model collects the water vapor given off during frying. I found the handle that lifts and lowers the basket a little too awkward to pull out, the knob for the temperature indicator too loose, and the safety lock stuck on occasion. No timer. Oil capacity: 8 to 10 cups. There is a 2-year warranty and the trilingual instruction pamphlet did not contain recipes, but did include an 800 customer service number.

T-FAL

Superclean Midi DeLuxe Deep Fryer, Model 3354. A lightweight, cool-to-the-touch model with a 1.5-pound capacity. The removable, nonstick, easy-clean tank features "lips" that extend out for easy lifting. The basket is easy to raise and lower with the handle. However, I feel the wire basket is too shallow. A removable, self-contained charcoal filter that can be used up to 40 times is located on the top of the lid under a vented cover, allowing steam to escape. There is a temperature pilot light, nonstick feet, and a thermostat adjustable from 1 to 5, with pictures as a gauge to frying temperature. It is therefore necessary to use a deep-fry thermometer to gauge the temperature of the oil. This deep fryer has minimum and maximum oil-level markers in the tank. The top of the fryer is removable for cleaning and is one of the easiest to take off and put on again. However, the area under the charcoal filter is difficult to clean. The lid opens too quickly when released and it is necessary to glove one hand with an oven mitt and catch the lid from the back while pushing the release button with the other hand. There is no cord storage or timer. The manufacturer's trilingual instruction booklet contains a picture guide of the machine and usage, and a troubleshooting guide but no recipes. There is a 1-year limited warranty and an authorized service center pamphlet is included with an 800 number.

Helpful Hints

1. Use the recommended frying temperature for each recipe. If the temperature is too low, the food will absorb too much oil. If the temperature is too high, the food will brown too quickly, and the interior will be undercooked.

2. Use a deep-fry thermometer to double-check the temperature of the oil. When frying in batches, allow the oil to return to the proper temperature before adding more food.

3. Choose a good-quality oil and one that is best suited for the type of food being fried. If using a solid vegetable shortening, follow the manufacturer's instruction booklet for proper usage.

4. There should be enough oil in the fryer to cover the food and permit easy circulation. Fill no more than one-third full and follow the manufacturer's guide for minimum and maximum levels.

5. Fry small amounts of food at a time. Crowding causes the temperature of the oil to decrease, increasing the frying time and the absorption of fat.

6. Dry foods thoroughly before adding to the hot oil to prevent the oil from splattering, "spitting," or foaming up. Also, dry foods well before coating in batter to help it adhere.

7. Lower foods gently into the hot oil with a fryer basket, a slotted metal spoon, metal tongs, or a metal pancake turner. Use a teaspoon or tablespoon to push batter or dough into the hot oil.

8. To turn foods in hot oil, use a slotted metal spoon, tongs, or a pancake turner rather than a fork or knife, which could puncture or disturb the protective coating.

9. Drain fried foods on a paper towel-lined tray. For economy, line the tray first with brown paper or newspaper. Change towels and paper as necessary.

10. Remove any small bits of food that float free in the oil during the cooking process.

11. If you plan to reuse the frying oil after frying, add a strip of lemon peel, a slice of potato, several slices of fresh ginger, or a bunch of thoroughly dried parsley to the oil to refresh it. (The fried parsley can be used as a garnish.) Then cool the oil completely and filter it through a funnel lined with a paper coffee filter. Store in a closed container and keep in a cool place or refrigerate.

12. When frying with reused oil, heat it slowly to allow any residual moisture to evaporate.

Useful Equipment

Deep-fat frying thermometer, for accurate temperature readings of the oil.

Instant-reading thermometer, for accurate temperature readings of poultry and meat.

Adjustable vegetable slicer with blades, for slicing chips and julienning vegetables.

Minute-second timer, for timing the cooking of foods.

Large fine-mesh strainer and paper coffee filters, for straining oil.

Slotted wide metal spatula, spoon, and tongs, for ease of placing food in the oil.

Crispy Appetizers and Snacks

Almost before they're out of the fryer, these eye-appealing and taste-tempting appetizers will disappear fast. There is something here for everyone and for every taste—an eclectic array of snacks and starters that will make for a great get-together no matter what the occasion.

If the gang's gathered around the TV for a bowl game, fortify your armchair quarterbacks with such happy-hour favorites as Cajun-Style Popcorn Shrimp, Fried Potato Skins with Cheddar Cheese and Bacon, and Buffalo Chicken Wings with all the trimmings. You will definitely score a touchdown. And with the deep fryer, cooking is so fast you'll even have time to watch the game.

The deep fryer can be a valuable helpmate in getting picky kids to eat a variety of foods. Teenagers won't be able to get enough Pigs in a Poke—savory cocktail franks wrapped in a crispy coating—or bite-size fried versions of a pizza-parlor favorite—calzones. For after-school munching or for a crunchy addition to a meal, fry up a batch of contemporary chips—sweet potato, yucca, or beet.

And if your guests are anything like mine, they like to gather where the action is—in the kitchen. So go beyond cheese and crackers with assorted appetizers and use the deep fryer to cook up quickly those ever-so-popular Chinese, Indian, Mexican, and Italian hot hor d'oeuvres so often ordered when dining out. Most, if not all, of the appetizers in this chapter can be prepared ahead of time, leaving only the frying for the last minute.

Hints and Tips

- Line a large baking sheet with several thicknesses of paper towels before you begin frying. Keep fried appetizers warm on a lined baking sheet in a preheated 250°F. oven while frying the remaining batches.

Buffalo Chicken Wings

These spicy fried chicken wings are said to have originated in Buffalo, New York. They quickly became a favorite in restaurants and bars all over the country. The addition of salad dressing mix to the dipping sauce is an idea I borrowed from my son Peter, who likes his wings hot! Serve these with cold beer to temper the fire.

MAKES 24 PIECES

24 whole chicken wings (about 4 pounds)
Solid vegetable shortening or oil for frying
4 tablespoons butter
¼ cup hot pepper sauce

1 tablespoon fresh lemon juice
2 teaspoons dry Italian salad dressing mix
Blue Cheese Dip (recipe follows)
Celery sticks

1. Cut off the tip of each chicken wing; discard or freeze for soup stock. Split each wing at the joint into 2 pieces. Rinse the chicken pieces with cold water and pat dry.
2. Place the shortening, in small pieces, in a deep fryer and melt, following the manufacturer's directions, or pour 2 inches of oil into a deep fryer. Heat to 375°F. Fry the wings, in batches without crowding, 12 to 15 minutes, until crisp and golden. Drain on paper towels.
3. In a small saucepan, melt the butter over medium heat. Stir in the hot sauce, lemon juice, and salad dressing mix. Heat just until bubbly.
4. Place the fried wings in a large bowl. Pour the hot butter sauce over the wings and toss to coat. To serve, mound the wings on a platter. Pass a bowl of Blue Cheese Dip and the celery sticks on the side.

Blue Cheese Dip

⅓ cup mayonnaise or creamy salad dressing

⅓ cup sour cream

⅓ cup crumbled blue cheese

1 garlic clove, crushed through a press

1 to 2 tablespoons milk

In a small bowl, combine all the ingredients. Stir to mix well. Cover and refrigerate at least 1 hour to mellow the flavors.

Mini Calzones

These savory, appetizer-size fried pies are easily made with prepared pizza dough. you can serve them plain or dipped into a mild spaghetti sauce.

MAKES 16 APPETIZERS

3 ounces mozzarella cheese, finely
  shredded (¾ cup)

1 ounce Genoa salami, finely chopped
  (¼ cup)

2 tablespoons freshly grated Romano
  cheese

1 tablespoon finely chopped fresh basil
  or 1 teaspoon dried

1 egg yolk

1 (10-ounce) tube refrigerated pizza
  crust dough

Olive or other vegetable oil for frying

Prepared spaghetti sauce, heated
  (optional)

1. In a small bowl, combine the mozzarella, salami, Romano cheese, basil, and egg yolk. Beat with a fork until well combined.

2. Unroll the pizza dough on a lightly floured work surface. Roll out the dough with a floured rolling pin to a 12-inch square. Even out the edges with a ruler. With a pizza cutter or small sharp knife, cut the dough into 16 (3-inch) squares.

3. Place 1½ level teaspoons of filling in the center of each square. Working with 1 square at a time, brush the edges of the dough lightly with water. Bring one corner of the dough over to enclose the filling, making a triangle; press the edges with the side of your thumb to seal. Gently press down in the center of the triangle to spread the filling.

4. Transfer the little calzones to the edge of the work surface with a wide spatula. Repeat with the remaining filling and dough. When all are done, press down on the edges of each with a floured fork; turn over and press again. Trim the edges with a pastry cutter or sharp knife. Place the calzones on a large baking sheet and set in the refrigerator while heating the oil.

5. Pour 1 inch of oil into a deep fryer. Heat to 350°F. Fry the calzones, 3 or 4 at a time, 1 minute on each side, until golden. Drain on paper towels. Serve warm, with heated spaghetti sauce for dipping, if desired.

Walnut-Crusted Fontina Sticks

Creamy melted cheese encased in a crusty nut coating makes a delectable hot hors d'oeuvre or snack. You can use any hard cheese, such as Cheddar, smoked Gouda, or Gruyère, or a softer cheese, such as mozzarella, Camembert, or Brie. Just make sure the cheese is well chilled. You can also serve these as a dessert course, surrounded with fruits of the season.

MAKES 18 TO 20 CHEESE STICKS

½ pound Italian fontina, Gruyère, or Cheddar cheese, in 1 piece, well chilled

⅓ cup ground walnuts

⅓ cup plain dry bread crumbs

1 egg

1 tablespoon all-purpose flour

Oil for frying

1. Preheat the oven to 250°F. Trim the rind from the cheese. Cut the cheese into 2½ × ½ × ½-inch sticks.

2. In a pie plate, toss the walnuts with the bread crumbs. In a shallow bowl, beat the egg until frothy.

3. Place the flour in a plastic food storage bag. Add the cheese sticks to the bag, a handful at a time, and dust with flour; shake any excess back into the bag. Dip the cheese sticks in the egg to coat throughly. Roll in the nut mixture, making sure each stick of cheese is completely coated. Place the sticks on a wire rack set over a baking sheet. Cover and refrigerate while heating the oil.

4. Pour 1 inch of oil into a deep fryer. Heat to 375°F. Fry the cheese sticks, in 3 batches, until golden, about 30 seconds. Drain on paper towels. Keep warm in the 250°F. oven while frying the remaining cheese sticks. Serve hot.

Yucca Chips

Yucca is shaped like a long, narrow sweet potato and is covered with a shiny, hard brown coat. Inside is a dense flesh, which looks like coconut. With the influence of Hispanic and Caribbean cooking, this vegetable is appearing in more and more supermarket produce departments. Try to buy a yucca that looks like a long, thick cucumber to get the chip shape for this recipe. You will need a vegetable slicer to cut this vegetable.

MAKES 4 SERVINGS

1-pound long, thick piece of yucca Coarse (kosher) salt
Oil for frying

1. Pare the yucca using a swivel-bladed vegetable peeler. Cut crosswise into thick chunks. Slice ⅛ inch thick on a vegetable slicer or mandoline. Pat dry between paper towels.

2. Pour 1½ inches of oil into a deep fryer. Heat to 350°F. Fry the yucca in batches, a handful at a time, until the yucca browns on the edges and is slightly tinged with brown in the center, about 2 minutes. Drain on paper towels. Sprinkle with salt while still warm.

Beet Chips

Vegetable chips, the latest rage in snack food eating, are appearing in supermarkets and health food stores and as garnishes in many upscale restaurants. These chips will be limp when taken out of the hot oil, but will crisp up upon cooling. It is important that you buy beets that are the same size for even frying.

MAKES 4 TO 6 SERVINGS

4 even-sized fresh beets (6 ounces each)
3 tablespoons cornstarch

Vegetable oil for frying
Coarse (kosher) salt

1. Trim the beets and pare with a swivel-bladed vegetable peeler. Slice ⅛ inch thick on a vegetable slicer or mandoline. Place the beet slices in a large bowl. Sprinkle the cornstarch over the beet slices and toss together with your fingers until coated.

2. Pour 1½ inches of oil into a deep fryer. Heat to 375°F. Fry the beets in a single layer in hot oil, until the beet slices begin to curl and darken slightly, about 3 to 4 minutes. Drain on paper towels. Sprinkle with salt while still warm.

VARIATION: Matchstick Beets: Cut the beets with the julienne plate of a vegetable slicer. Prepare as above. Fry a handful at a time for 3 to 4 minutes. Drain on paper towels. Sprinkle with salt while still warm.

Saratoga Chips

Potato chips have been known to exist since the 1840s, but they were originally fairly thick. Thin crisp chips as we know them are said to have begun at a spa for the wealthy in Saratoga Springs, New York. The story goes that an irate diner returned his fried potatoes saying they were too thick. To placate the diner, Chef George Crum sliced the potatoes very thin, fried them up, and returned them to the table. They were so well received that the next day, they were given out free, in paper cups, at the bar.

MAKES 4 SERVINGS

4 large baking potatoes, such as Russets or Idahos (8 ounces each), peeled

Salt

Oil for frying

1. Set a mandoline or vegetable slicer blade to 1/16 inch thick. Slice the potatoes into rounds and immediately place in a bowl of cold water. When all the potatoes are sliced, drain off the water. (This removes the starch from the potatoes.) Re-cover the potatoes with fresh water, adding 1 teaspoon salt and 4 cups of water. Add 8 to 12 ice cubes. Let stand 1 hour at room temperature.

2. Pour 1½ inches of oil into a deep fryer. Heat to 330°F. Drain the potatoes and roll in clean kitchen towels to dry thoroughly. (This is important to prevent the oil from spattering and bubbling over.)

3. Divide the potatoes into 4 batches. Place 1 batch in a fryer basket and gently lower into the hot oil, which will bubble up, so be careful. Fry 2 to 3 minutes, until very pale gold in color, but do not brown. Drain on paper towels. Repeat with the remaining potatoes. This first frying can be done earlier in the day.

4. Just before serving, heat the oil to 360° to 365°F. Fry half the potatoes, 1 to 2 minutes, until crisp and golden brown. Drain on paper towels. Repeat with the remaining potatoes. Sprinkle with salt to taste and serve at once.

Sweet Potato Chips

For even frying, buy sweet potatoes of the same size and shape. I chose fat, chunky potatoes that fit in the palm of my hand. You have to watch carefully that the potatoes don't brown too much; they should be slightly colored at the edges and still orange in the center. The potatoes are slightly soft when they come out of the oil, but they will crisp up upon cooling.

MAKES 4 SERVINGS

2 sweet potatoes (5 ounces each),
  peeled

Oil for frying
Coarse (kosher) salt

1. Slice the sweet potatoes ⅛ inch thick on a vegetable slicer or mandoline. Pat dry with paper towels.

2. Pour 1 inch of oil into a deep fryer. Heat to 350°F. Fry a handful of sweet potato slices at a time just until lightly browned at the edges but still orange in the center, about 2 minutes. Drain on paper towels. Repeat until all the chips are cooked. Sprinkle with salt to taste and serve at once.

Fried Potato Skins with
Cheddar Cheese and Bacon

This popular finger food has been the rage ever since it first started appearing on restaurant menus. My version uses a ready-prepared bacon, which eliminates the need for cooking the bacon. Look for it in supermarkets. Save the potato pulp for hash browns or mashed potatoes.

MAKES 16 PIECES

4 large baking potatoes (8 ounces each), about 5 to 5½ inches long
Oil
3 tablespoons all-purpose flour
1 cup shredded sharp Cheddar cheese

4 slices of hickory-flavor ready-cooked bacon, chopped
¼ cup sour cream
¼ cup coarsely chopped scallions

1. Preheat the oven to 450°F. Scrub and dry the potatoes well. Lightly brush with oil. Place directly on the rack in the oven and bake 45 minutes, or until fork-tender. Let cool. Raise the oven temperature to broil.

2. Cut the potatoes lengthwise into quarters and scoop out the pulp, leaving a ¼-inch shell. Place the flour in a plastic food storage bag. Add the potato skins in batches and shake to coat with flour.

3. Pour 1 inch of oil into a deep fryer. Heat to 375°F. Fry the potato skins in batches, 3 to 4 at a time, for 1½ to 2 minutes, until golden and crisp. Drain on paper towels.

4. Place the fried potato skins, cut-sides up, on a shallow baking pan. Sprinkle the cheese and bacon evenly over the potato skins. Place under the broiler and heat for about 1 minute to melt the cheese. Top with a dollop of sour cream and scallions. Serve at once.

Beef Satay with Peanut Sauce

Indonesian in origin, satay *is believed to be a corruption of the word* steak. *Nowadays it is any food that is cooked on a skewer and served with a flavorful sauce. To make this dish, you'll need 48 (6-inch) bamboo skewers that have been soaked in cold water for 30 minutes to prevent burning.*

MAKES 48 PIECES

1 pound beef flank steak
4 scallions, cut into 1-inch pieces
3 garlic cloves
1 quarter-size slice of peeled fresh
 ginger
1 small jalapeño pepper, seeded and
 minced

2 teaspoons cornstarch
¼ cup fresh lime juice
1 tablespoon peanut or other vegetable
 oil, plus oil for frying
Peanut Sauce (recipe follows)

1. Place the steak in the freezer on a metal baking sheet and freeze at least 2 hours to firm up; this makes for easier slicing. When the meat is hard enough, trim off as much visible fat as possible. With a sharp knife, cut the beef crosswise on an angle into ⅛-inch-thick slices. Place the meat in a medium bowl.

2. In a food processor, combine the scallions, garlic, ginger, jalapeño pepper, cornstarch, lime juice, and 1 tablespoon oil. Process in pulses until pureed. Pour over the beef and toss to coat. Let stand 30 minutes at room temperature or no longer than 1 hour in the refrigerator (any longer and the meat will fall apart).

3. Thread 1 piece of meat onto each skewer, straightening the slices so they lie flat and making sure the ends are securely fastened.

4. Pour 1 inch of oil into a deep fryer. Heat to 375°F. Fry in batches of 5 or 6 skewers at a time, 30 to 40 seconds, just until the meat is lightly browned around the edges. Drain briefly on paper towels. Serve hot, with Peanut Sauce for dipping.

Peanut Sauce

Besides being perfect for all kinds of satays, try this sauce as a dip for crisp fresh vegetables or thin it out slightly and serve as a dressing with a tofu and vegetable pita.

MAKES 1 CUP

2 scallions, cut into 1-inch pieces
¼ cup loosely packed fresh cilantro
1 quarter-size slice of peeled fresh
    ginger
1 tablespoon sugar
½ cup creamy or chunky peanut
    butter

⅓ cup unsweetened coconut milk or
    heavy cream
1½ tablespoons soy sauce
¼ teaspoon cayenne
1 tablespoon fresh lime juice

1. Place the scallions, cilantro, ginger, and sugar in a food processor. Process in pulses until finely chopped. Add the peanut butter, coconut milk, soy sauce, cayenne, and lime juice. Puree until smooth.

2. Pour the peanut sauce into a small bowl. If it is too thick for dipping, stir in a little more coconut milk or heavy cream. Serve at room temperature.

Chinese Shrimp Toast

When you spread the shrimp paste over the toast here, make sure it covers the bread completely so the edges don't burn during frying. Since stale bread absorbs less oil than fresh, let the slices air-dry overnight on a wire rack.

MAKES 24 PIECES

½ pound fresh shrimp, shelled and deveined

¼ cup finely chopped water chestnuts

2 tablespoons finely chopped scallions

1 teaspoon finely shredded peeled fresh ginger

1 egg

1 tablespoon cornstarch

1 teaspoon salt

½ teaspoon sugar

Pinch of cayenne

½ teaspoon Asian sesame oil (optional)

6 slices of stale white bread

Peanut or other vegetable oil for frying

1. Rinse the shrimp under cold water. Pat dry with paper towels.

2. Place the shrimp in a food processor. Add the water chestnuts, scallions, and ginger. Process in pulses until the shrimp is paste. Add the egg, cornstarch, salt, sugar, cayenne, and sesame oil. Process in pulses until combined. Turn into a bowl.

3. Trim the crusts off the bread. Spread 2½ level tablespoons of shrimp paste over each slice to cover completely. Cut each slice diagonally into 4 triangles with a sharp knife that has been dipped in warm water, which prevents the shrimp paste from adhering to the knife. Place the triangles on a baking sheet and refrigerate while heating the oil. Preheat the oven to 250°F.

4. Pour 1½ inches of oil into a deep fryer. Heat to 375°F. Carefully slide 4 or 5 bread triangles, shrimp-side down, into the hot oil. Fry 1 minute. Turn with a slotted spoon and fry 10 seconds longer, or until the bread is golden. Drain on paper towels. Keep warm in the oven while frying the remaining toasts. Serve hot.

Crispy Appetizers and Snacks

Coconut Shrimp

Unsweetened shredded coconut is available in health food stores and Indian markets. The unsweetened milk comes in cans, which are in Asian markets and in many supermarkets.

MAKES 4 TO 6 SERVINGS

1 pound large shrimp
¼ cup all-purpose flour
½ teaspoon dry mustard
½ teaspoon salt
½ cup unsweetened shredded coconut
¼ cup plain dry bread crumbs

2 eggs
¼ cup unsweetened coconut milk or heavy cream
Oil for frying
Bottled Chinese duck sauce or plum chutney

1. Shell and devein the shrimp under cold water, leaving the tails on. Pat the shrimp dry with paper towels.

2. On a sheet of wax paper, combine the flour, dry mustard, and salt. Stir with a fork to mix. Combine the coconut and bread crumbs on another sheet of wax paper; toss to mix. In a pie plate, beat the eggs with the coconut milk or cream until well blended.

3. Dredge the shrimp in the seasoned flour; shake off any excess. Dip in the egg mixture and dredge in the coconut crumbs to coat completely. Place the shrimp on a wire rack set over a large baking sheet. Chill in the refrigerator while heating the oil.

4. Pour 1½ inches of oil into a deep fryer. Heat to 375°F. Fry the shrimp in batches, 3 or 4 at a time, 2 to 4 minutes, until golden brown, turning once. Drain on paper towels. Serve warm, with duck sauce or chutney for dipping.

Quesadillas

½ pound Monterey Jack with jalapeño chile peppers, plain Monterey Jack, Colby, or Muenster cheese

1½ cups masa harina (finely ground cornmeal)

½ cup all-purpose flour

1 teaspoon baking powder

½ teaspoon salt

2 teaspoons ground cumin

¾ to 1 cup warm tap water

Oil for frying

Fresh Tomato Salsa (page 80) or prepared salsa

1. Cut the cheese into 1 × ¼ × ¼-inch sticks. Divide into 24 stacks, about 4 or 5 pieces each, and place the stacks on a baking sheet. Cover with plastic wrap to prevent drying out.

2. In a medium bowl, combine the masa harina, flour, baking powder, salt, and cumin. Stir with a fork or whisk to mix. Add ¾ cup of warm water and stir until moistened. Add as much of the remaining water, 1 tablespoon at a time, as needed to make the mixture come together; it should not be wet or sticky. Gather the dough together and shape into a slightly flattened ball. Cut into 24 equal wedges and lightly press each into an irregular ball. Keep the dough covered with plastic wrap to prevent drying out.

3. Place 1 piece of dough between 2 sheets of wax paper. Press down with the bottom of a pie plate to flatten to a 3½-inch round. Use a rolling pin, if necessary, to reach the desired diameter. (If you have a tortilla press, by all means use it.) Carefully lift off the top piece of wax paper. Flip over and peel off the other piece of paper. Place the tortilla on a large baking sheet and cover. Repeat with the remaining dough.

4. Forming 1 quesadilla at a time, place 1 cheese stack in the center of each tortilla. Fold 1 edge over the cheese to meet the opposite edge and form a half-moon shape. Pinch to seal; press with the tines of a fork to secure. Place on a large baking sheet and keep covered. Preheat the oven to 250°F.

5. Pour ¾ to 1 inch of oil into a deep fryer. Heat to 375°F. Fry the quesadillas in batches, 4 or 5 at a time, 1½ to 2 minutes, or until golden, turning once. Drain on paper towels. Keep warm in the oven while frying the remaining quesadillas. Serve hot with Fresh Tomato Salsa or your favorite brand of salsa.

Sweet Potato Samosas with Cilantro Cream

Good things come in small packages—such as these mildly spiced samosas, a common Indian snack. I like to pass them as a hot hors d'oeuvre at cocktail parties. Self-rising flour makes an easy, foolproof pastry, which encloses a lively curried sweet potato filling spiked with jalapeño pepper and fresh ginger.

MAKES 16 SAMOSAS

1¼ cups self-rising flour
3 tablespoons curry powder
¼ cup solid vegetable shortening
3 to 4 tablespoons ice water
1 (15- to 16-ounce) can sweet
   potatoes, drained

1 tablespoon minced seeded pickled
   jalapeño pepper
1 teaspoon grated fresh ginger
Shortening or oil for frying
Cilantro Cream (recipe follows)

1. In a large bowl, mix the flour with 1 tablespoon of the curry powder. Cut in the shortening with a pastry blender or 2 knives used scissor fashion until the mixture resembles coarse crumbs. Sprinkle the ice water over the top and mix lightly with a fork just until the pastry is evenly moistened but not sticky. Gather the dough into a ball. Cover with plastic wrap and set aside at room temperature.

2. In a food processor, combine the drained sweet potatoes with the pickled jalapeño pepper, ginger, and remaining 2 tablespoons curry powder. Process in pulses until the filling is smooth. You may have to turn off the processor and scrape down the sides of the container once or twice. Transfer the sweet potato filling to a small bowl. You should have 1 cup.

3. On a lightly floured surface, roll out the pastry to noodle thickness (¹⁄₁₆ inch) with a floured rolling pin. Cut into rounds with a floured 4-inch round cutter (or use the plastic top from a 1-pound coffee can, cutting around the top with the point of a sharp knife). Remove the trimmings from around the circles. Set the pastry rounds on a baking sheet. Reroll the trimmings to make additional rounds.

4. Place 1 level tablespoon of the sweet potato filling in the center of each pastry round. Lightly moisten the edges of the dough with water. Fold the pastry over the filling to form a half-moon shape. Pinch lightly to seal. Press with the floured tines of a fork; turn the samosas over and press again. Trim the edges neatly with a pastry cutter or sharp knife.

5. Pour 1 inch of melted shortening or oil into a deep fryer. Heat to 375°F. Fry the samosas in batches, 3 to 5 at a time, 2 minutes, or until light golden. Drain on paper towels. Serve warm, with Cilantro Cream for dipping.

Cilantro Cream

1 cup plain yogurt
1 tablespoon finely chopped fresh
  cilantro

1 tablespoon fresh lime juice
½ teaspoon grated fresh lime zest
Pinch of sugar (optional)

In a small bowl, combine all the ingredients. Stir to mix well. Cover and refrigerate at least 1 hour for the flavors to mellow.

Pigs in a Poke

Next time you have a cocktail party, try these cocktail franks cloaked in a beer batter and deep-fried. They are sure to go fast. The number of tiny frankfurters will vary in a 12-ounce package, but there are usually 24 to 26.

MAKES 24 TO 26 APPETIZERS

½ cup plus 2 tablespoons self-rising
   flour
½ cup flat beer
1 tablespoon vegetable oil
1 (12-ounce) package beef cocktail
   franks

1 egg white
Oil for frying
Spicy mustard

1. In a medium bowl, whisk together the flour, beer, and 1 tablespoon oil. Let the batter stand at room temperature 1 hour.

2. Pat the franks dry with paper towels. Insert a wooden toothpick halfway into 1 end of each frank. Pour 1 inch of oil into a deep fryer. Heat to 375°F.

3. In a small bowl, beat the egg white until stiff peaks form. Fold into the beer batter. Pour the batter into a 2-cup glass measure (this makes for easier dipping of the franks).

4. One at a time, holding onto the toothpick as a handle, twirl a frank in the batter, letting the excess drip back into the measure. Immediately slide the frank into the hot oil. Fry in batches, 5 or 6 at a time, 2½ minutes, or until the crust is golden brown, turning once halfway through to cook evenly. Drain on paper towels. Keep warm while frying the remaining franks. Serve hot, with spicy mustard for dipping.

Cajun-Style Popcorn Shrimp

Popcorn shrimp refers to the shape of the shrimp after frying—like a popped kernel of corn. Serve with a squeeze of lemon or your favorite seafood dipping sauce.

MAKES 4 APPETIZER SERVINGS

1 pound small shrimp, peeled and
   deveined
1 egg
1 teaspoon salt
1 teaspoon cayenne
½ teaspoon garlic powder

¼ teaspoon dried leaf thyme
¼ teaspoon dried oregano
⅛ teaspoon pepper
½ cup all-purpose flour
¾ to 1 cup cornmeal
Oil for frying

1. Rinse the shrimp under cold water. Pat dry with paper towels.

2. In a medium bowl, beat the egg with the salt, cayenne, garlic powder, thyme, oregano, and black pepper until frothy. On separate sheets of wax paper, place the flour and cornmeal.

3. Dredge the shrimp in the flour. Dip in the seasoned egg mixture and coat in the cornmeal, using a fork. Place the shrimp on a wire rack set over a baking sheet. Repeat until all the shrimp are coated.

4. Pour 1½ inches of oil into a deep fryer. Heat to 375°F. Fry the shrimp in batches for 1 to 2 minutes, until the crust is golden and the shrimp curl and turn pink. Drain on paper towels. Serve hot.

Zesty Tex-Mex Fried Won Tons

These savory pop-in-the-mouth appetizers will disappear fast. They can be frozen and reheated, loosely covered, in a 350°F. oven for 10 to 12 minutes.

MAKES 34 TO 36 APPETIZERS

½ pound lean ground beef or turkey

¼ cup chopped onion

¼ cup chopped green bell pepper

1 (8-ounce) can refried beans

¼ cup shredded sharp Cheddar cheese
  or Monterey Jack cheese with
  jalapeño chile peppers

1 tablespoon spicy ketchup

2 teaspoons chili powder

½ teaspoon ground cumin

¼ teaspoon salt

34 to 36 (3-inch) won ton skins

Oil for frying

Bottled taco sauce

1. In a large skillet over medium heat, cook the beef, onion, and green pepper until the beef has browned and the vegetables are soft, about 4 minutes. Drain off any fat. Stir in the beans, cheese, ketchup, chili powder, cumin, and salt.

2. Working with 1 won ton skin at a time (keep the remaining skins covered to prevent drying out), place the won ton with 1 point facing you. Spoon 2 level teaspoons of the filling onto the lower third of the won ton. Fold the bottom point of the skin up over the filling and tuck it under the filling. Moisten the remaining edges lightly with water. Fold in the sides to form an envelope and roll up. Press the edge to seal. Place, seam-side down, on a large baking sheet; cover to prevent drying out. Repeat with the remaining won ton skins and filling.

3. Pour 1½ inches of oil into a deep fryer. Heat to 375°F. Fry the won tons, 5 at a time, about 2 minutes, until crispy and brown, turning once. Drain on paper towels. Keep warm. Repeat with the remaining won tons. Serve hot, with taco sauce for dipping.

Vegetable Egg Rolls

Egg roll wrappers are made with wheat flour, whereas spring roll wrappers are made with rice flour. You can switch the wrappers if one is easier to find than the other. Both can be purchased in Asian markets and in the refrigerated or frozen sections of some supermarkets.

MAKES 8 EGG ROLLS

---

4 large dried Chinese black
   mushrooms
1 tablespoon peanut or other vegetable
   oil, plus oil for frying
1 tablespoon minced fresh garlic
1 tablespoon minced fresh ginger
2 cups shredded Savoy or ordinary
   green cabbage
1 cup shredded fresh spinach
½ cup julienned fresh snow peas

½ cup shredded carrots
½ cup thinly sliced scallions
2 tablespoons minced fresh cilantro
½ teaspoon salt
⅛ teaspoon pepper
1 egg
8 egg roll wrappers
Chinese Mustard Sauce (recipe follows)
Apricot Dipping Sauce (page 39)

1. In a small bowl, soak the mushrooms in warm water 20 minutes, or until soft. Drain the mushrooms and squeeze out excess water. Remove the stems and cut the mushrooms into thin strips.

2. In a large skillet, heat 1 tablespoon of the oil. Add the garlic and ginger; stir-fry 1 minute. Add the cabbage, spinach, snow peas, carrots, and scallions. Stir-fry 2 to 3 minutes, or until the vegetables are wilted. Stir in the cilantro, salt, and pepper. Remove from the heat and let cool.

3. In a small cup, beat the egg well. When working with the egg roll wrappers, keep them covered to prevent drying out. For each egg roll, place 1 wrapper with 1 corner facing you. Place ¼ cup of the cooled filling slightly off center and spread the filling to a 3-inch length. Using a pastry brush, brush the edges of the wrapper with the beaten egg. Fold the corner nearest you over the filling and roll halfway up. Fold the sides of the wrapper in over the filling like an envelope, and finish rolling up. Place seam-side down on a wax paper-lined tray and cover with plastic wrap to prevent drying out. Repeat with the remaining egg roll wrappers and filling. The egg rolls can be prepared to this point and refrigerated for up to 3 hours until ready to fry.

4. Pour 1½ inches of oil into a deep fryer. Heat to 365°F. Fry 2 egg rolls at a time, 1½ minutes on each side, until golden brown. Drain on paper towels. Serve hot, with the Chinese Mustard Sauce and Apricot Dipping Sauce for dipping.

Chinese Mustard Sauce

This sauce is hot, *and a little goes a long way.*

MAKES ABOUT ⅓ CUP

¼ cup dry mustard

¼ cup water

2 teaspoons vegetable oil

¼ teaspoon salt

In a small bowl, whisk together the mustard, water, vegetable oil, and salt until smooth. Let stand at room temperature 20 minutes, or longer if desired. The longer the mustard stands, the hotter it gets.

Apricot Dipping Sauce

MAKES ½ CUP

½ cup apricot or peach preserves
3 tablespoons rice wine vinegar

1½ teaspoons minced fresh ginger

In a small saucepan, combine the preserves, vinegar, and ginger. Cook over low heat, stirring constantly, until the preserves are melted and the sauce is smooth. Let cool to room temperature before serving.

Just Fried Chicken

Crispy, finger-lickin' fried chicken stands or falls with the cook, and everyone declares their recipe is the best. Whether it is cooked in vegetable shortening, olive oil, or lard; marinated in buttermilk or soaked in cold water; dipped in batter, dredged in flour only, or in flour, beaten egg, and crumbs; heavily spiced or seasoned with salt and pepper, fried chicken comes through with flying colors in the deep fryer.

Covered fryers eliminate the spattering and sputtering of oil, and charcoal filters reduce the odor of frying fat. Wire fryer baskets make lifting and lowering the chicken into the hot fat easy. With an automatic thermostat, you know the temperature is being maintained. And cleanup is a breeze no matter what deep fryer you have. What you will get when frying in the deep fryer is a piece of crisp, fried chicken that is moist and juicy inside.

Check the manufacturer's manual for melting solid vegetable shortening in the machine. One might tell you to melt it in small pieces in the deep fryer, whereas another manufacturer may have you melt it over low heat in a heavy saucepan, then carefully pour it into the deep fryer. A 48-ounce can of solid shortening will melt down to 7 cups. Fill the deep fryer to the maximum level mark or no more than one-third full.

Small birds of no more than 3 pounds fry up most successfully.

Always dry coated chicken pieces on a wire rack to set the coating before frying. A temperature setting between 340° to 360°F. works best. Any higher and the coating burns and the chicken is not cooked through. To make sure the chicken pieces are done, an instant-reading thermometer is your best guide. The internal temperature of a fully cooked piece of chicken should be 180°F. Try not to test the chicken pieces with a knife to see if the juices run clear. If the chicken is not done you will have to return it to the hot oil, which increases the fat absorption of the piece.

Hints and Tips

- You can substitute an equal weight of thighs and drumsticks for a cut-up broiler-fryer chicken if your family likes just dark meat. Select thighs and drumsticks that do not weigh more than 5 ounces each.
- Skinning the chicken pieces is optional.
- To save money, you can cut up the chicken yourself. Save the backbones to make soup stock.
- Keep fried chicken warm in a 250°F. oven between batches.
- Fried chicken is best served hot or cooled to room temperature. If refrigerated, the crisp crust will soften.

Double-Dipped Fried Chicken

This is my favorite way of preparing fried chicken. To make it taste really good, you need to season it with generous amounts of salt and black pepper. The double-coating method suggested here creates a nice crisp crust. Refrigerating softens the crust, so fry up the chicken just before you are ready to serve it.

MAKES 4 SERVINGS

1 egg
¼ cup seltzer, club soda, or water
1½ teaspoons salt
1½ teaspoons pepper
1½ teaspoons garlic powder

1 (3-pound) broiler-fryer chicken, cut up, with breasts halved
2 cups all-purpose flour
Solid vegetable shortening or oil for frying

1. In a large bowl, whisk together the egg, seltzer, and 1 teaspoon *each* salt, pepper, and garlic powder. Add the chicken pieces and turn to coat thoroughly. Let stand 15 minutes, turning occasionally.

2. In a large plastic food storage bag, mix the flour with the remaining ½ teaspoon each salt, pepper, and garlic powder. Remove the chicken pieces from the egg, 1 piece at a time, letting the excess drip off back into the bowl. Place 1 or 2 pieces of chicken in the plastic bag and shake to coat all over with the seasoned flour. Place the coated chicken on a wire rack set over a baking sheet. When all of the chicken pieces have been coated, redip them in the egg mixture and then shake them in the seasoned flour a second time. Return to the wire rack. Let stand at room temperature 30 minutes to set the coating.

3. Place the shortening in small pieces in a deep fryer and melt, following the manufacturer's directions, or pour in 1½ inches of oil. Heat to 350°F. Fry the chicken in batches, a few pieces at a time, until golden brown: breast halves, wings, and thighs will take 10 to 12 minutes; drumsticks will take 8 to 10 minutes (to an internal temperature of 180°F.). Drain on paper towels. Serve warm.

Buttermilk Fried Chicken

Buttermilk tenderizes the chicken while it produces a fine, crisp crust with excellent flavor.

MAKES 4 SERVINGS

1 (3-pound) broiler-fryer chicken, cut up, with breasts halved
1 cup buttermilk
2 teaspoons salt
1½ teaspoons hot Hungarian paprika
¾ teaspoon pepper
1 cup self-rising flour
Solid vegetable shortening or oil for frying

1. Arrange the chicken pieces in a single layer in a shallow baking dish. Pour the buttermilk over the chicken. Cover and refrigerate 1 hour, turning once.

2. Transfer the chicken pieces to a large baking sheet; discard the buttermilk. In a small bowl, combine the salt, paprika, and pepper. Rub 2 teaspoons of this seasoning mixture into the chicken pieces.

3. Place the remaining seasoning mixture in a large plastic food storage bag with the flour and shake to mix. Place 1 or 2 pieces of chicken in the bag and shake to coat all over. Place on a wire rack set over a baking sheet. Let stand at room temperature 30 minutes to set the coating.

4. Place the shortening in small pieces in a deep fryer and melt, following the manufacturer's directions, or pour in 1½ inches of oil. Heat to 350°F. Fry the chicken in batches, a few pieces at time, until golden brown: breast halves, wings, and thighs will take 10 to 12 minutes; drumsticks will take 8 to 10 minutes (to an internal temperature of 180°F.). Drain on paper towels. Serve warm.

Tex-Mex Chicken Cutlets with Fresh Tomato Vinaigrette

Chicken cutlets are so versatile, they take well to many different seasonings. With the herb and spice blend that goes into this coating, you end up with very tasty chicken that can be served as cutlets, as suggested below, or cut into strips and tucked into warmed pitas with lettuce, tomato, and onion, or covered with Monterey Jack and placed under a hot broiler to melt the cheese.

MAKES 4 SERVINGS

4 skinless, boneless chicken breast halves (5 to 6 ounces each)
1 teaspoon salt
¼ teaspoon pepper
3 to 4 tablespoons all-purpose flour
¾ cup unseasoned dry bread crumbs
2 eggs
2 teaspoons dried oregano

2 teaspoons ground coriander
1½ teaspoons ground cumin
1 teaspoon chili powder
½ teaspoon cayenne
Solid vegetable shortening or oil for frying
Fresh Tomato Vinaigrette (recipe follows)

1. Remove the tenderloins from the chicken breasts and reserve for another use. Pound each piece of chicken between 2 sheets of wax paper to a ⅜-inch thickness. Season with the salt and pepper.

2. Place the flour and bread crumbs on separate sheets of wax paper. In a pie plate, beat the eggs with the oregano, coriander, cumin, chili powder, and cayenne with a fork to make a thin paste.

3. Working with 1 piece at a time, dredge the chicken breasts in the flour, dip into the egg mixture, and roll in the bread crumbs to coat thoroughly. Place on a wire rack set over a baking sheet. Let stand at room temperature 15 minutes to set the coating.

4. Place the shortening in small pieces in a deep fryer and melt, following the manufacturer's directions, or pour in 1½ inches of oil. Heat to 360°F. Fry the cutlets, 1 at a time, 2 minutes, until golden. Drain on paper towels. Keep warm while frying the remaining chicken. Serve with Fresh Tomato Vinaigrette.

Fresh Tomato Vinaigrette

½ teaspoon whole cumin seeds

3 large plum tomatoes, seeded and cut into ½-inch dice

2 teaspoons minced seeded pickled jalapeño pepper

2 tablespoons olive oil

2 tablespoons red wine vinegar

1 tablespoon minced fresh cilantro

1. In a small dry skillet, toast the cumin seeds over low heat, stirring, until fragrant, about 5 minutes. Pour into a small bowl.

2. Add the tomatoes, pickled jalapeño pepper, olive oil, vinegar, and cilantro. Mix well. Serve cold or at room temperature.

Cajun-Style Chicken Nuggets with Honey Mustard Dip

1 pound skinless, boneless chicken
  breast halves
½ teaspoon salt
½ teaspoon pepper
1 egg
⅓ cup seltzer, club soda, or water
⅓ cup all-purpose flour

1½ teaspoons cayenne
1½ teaspoons onion powder
1 teaspoon dried thyme leaves
1 teaspoon garlic powder
Solid vegetable shortening or oil for
  frying
Honey Mustard Dip (recipe follows)

1. Remove the tenderloins from the chicken breasts. Cut both the tenderloins and chicken breasts into 1½-inch pieces. Season with the salt and pepper.

2. In a pie plate, beat the egg with the seltzer. Add the chicken pieces and turn to coat. Let stand at room temperature 15 minutes, turning once or twice.

3. On wax paper, mix the flour, cayenne, onion powder, thyme, and garlic powder. Lift the chicken pieces from the egg mixture a few at a time; let the excess drip back onto the plate. Place in the seasoned flour and toss between 2 forks to coat. Place the chicken pieces on a wire rack set over a baking sheet. When all the chicken pieces are coated, redip in the egg mixture, then in the seasoned flour. If you run short, pour any flour that accumulates on the baking sheet back onto the wax paper. Let the chicken stand on the wire rack 15 minutes to set the coating.

4. Place the shortening in small pieces in a deep fryer and melt, following the manufacturer's directions, or pour in 1½ inches of oil. Heat to 360°F. Place 5 or 6 pieces of chicken in the wire basket and lower into the hot fat. Fry 5 minutes, or until golden brown. Drain on paper towels. Keep warm while frying the remaining batches of chicken. Serve hot or warm, with Honey Mustard Dip.

Honey Mustard Dip

This dip is also good with raw or lightly cooked vegetables, as a salad dressing for greens, or as a spread for poultry, pork, or ham sandwiches.

MAKES ⅔ CUP

⅓ cup mayonnaise or creamy salad dressing

3 tablespoons Dijon mustard
3 tablespoons honey

In a small bowl, whisk together all the ingredients.

Southern Fried Chicken with Cream Gravy

There are as many versions of this dish as there are cooks. It teams well with mashed potatoes.

MAKES 4 SERVINGS

1 (3-pound) broiler-fryer chicken, cut up, with breasts halved
1½ tablespoons salt
½ cup all-purpose flour
¾ teaspoon pepper
¾ teaspoon cayenne
½ teaspoon dried thyme leaves
Solid vegetable shortening or oil for frying
Cream Gravy (recipe follows)

1. In a large bowl, combine the chicken pieces, 4 cups of cold water, and 1 tablespoon of the salt. Cover and refrigerate at least 2 hours. Drain the chicken.

2. In a large plastic food storage bag, combine the flour with the pepper, cayenne, thyme, and remaining 1½ teaspoons salt. Shake to mix. Remove 2 tablespoons seasoned flour and set aside for the gravy.

3. Place the chicken pieces in the bag, a few at a time, and shake to coat all over. Place on a wire rack set over a baking sheet. Let stand at room temperature 30 minutes to set the coating.

4. Place the shortening in small pieces in a deep fryer and melt, following the manufacturer's directions, or pour in 1½ inches of oil. Heat the oil to 360°F. Fry the chicken in batches, a few pieces at a time, until golden brown: breast, wings, and thighs will take 10 to 12 minutes; drumsticks will take 8 to 10 minutes (to an internal temperature of 180°F.). Drain on paper towels. Serve hot. Pass a sauceboat of Cream Gravy on the side.

Cream Gravy

A little of the shortening or oil from frying the chicken is used to make this gravy. Be sure to remove it from the deep fryer with a metal ladle, then measure it with a metal measuring spoon, as plastic will melt.

MAKES 1 CUP

2 tablespoons melted shortening or oil (left over from frying chicken)

2 tablespoons seasoned flour, reserved from Southern Fried Chicken with Cream Gravy (preceding recipe)

1 cup light cream

1. In a small saucepan, heat the melted shortening or oil over medium-low heat. Whisk in the seasoned flour. Cook, stirring, 1 to 2 minutes without browning.

2. Gradually stir in the cream. Bring to a boil, whisking until thickened and smooth, about 2 minutes.

Garlic-Fried Drumsticks

Here drumsticks are marinated overnight in garlicky spiced buttermilk to gather flavor. These are good hot or cold

2 cups buttermilk

4 garlic cloves, crushed through a
  press

2 teaspoons salt

2 teaspoons pepper

2 teaspoons cayenne

12 chicken drumsticks, 3 to 4 ounces
  each (about 2½ pounds)

¾ cup all-purpose flour

Solid vegetable shortening or oil for
  frying

1. In a large bowl, whisk together the buttermilk, garlic, and 1½ teaspoons each of the salt, pepper, and cayenne. Add the drumsticks and turn to coat. Cover and refrigerate overnight, turning occasionally.

2. In a large plastic food storage bag, combine the flour with the remaining ½ teaspoon each salt, pepper, and cayenne; shake to mix. Lift the chicken pieces from the buttermilk, 1 at a time, letting the excess drip back into the bowl. Add 1 or 2 drumsticks at a time to the seasoned flour and shake to coat. Place on a wire rack set over a baking sheet. Let stand at room temperature 30 minutes to set the coating. Discard the buttermilk.

3. Place the shortening in small pieces in a deep fryer and melt, following the manufacturer's directions, or pour 1½ inches of oil into a deep fryer. Heat to 340°F. Fry 3 or 4 drumsticks at a time, turning once, until golden brown, 12 to 15 minutes (to an internal temperature of 180°F.). Drain on paper towels. Serve hot.

Southwestern-Style Chicken Pillows

Chicken breasts are wrapped around Monterey Jack cheese, then coated with a cumin and chili powder cornmeal crust. For extra heat, substitute jack cheese flavored with habanero chiles. The stuffed chicken will turn golden before it is completely cooked through, so be sure to cook it long enough. These are good topped with guacamole and sour cream.

MAKES 4 SERVINGS

4 large skinless, boneless chicken breast halves (7½ to 8 ounces each)

4 ounces coarsely shredded Monterey Jack cheese with jalapeño peppers

2 tablespoons chopped fresh oregano or 2 teaspoons dried

⅓ cup yellow cornmeal

1½ teaspoons chili powder

½ teaspoon ground cumin

3 tablespoons all-purpose flour

1 egg

Solid vegetable shortening or oil for frying

Tomato-Avocado Salsa (recipe follows)

1. Remove the tenderloins from the chicken breasts and reserve for another use. Trim off any excess fat. Place each chicken breast, smooth-side up, between 2 sheets of wax paper and pound with a mallet or the flat side of a cleaver to a ¼-inch thickness, being careful not to tear the chicken. Turn the chicken over so the rough side is up.
2. Place one-fourth of the cheese in the center of each chicken breast. Sprinkle each with 1½ teaspoons of the fresh oregano or ½ teaspoon dried. Bring one long end of the chicken breast up over the cheese, fold in the sides, and roll up tightly, making sure no cheese is showing; fasten with wooden toothpicks. You should have a chicken pillow about 4½ × 1½ inches. Place, rounded-side up, on a baking sheet. Repeat with the remaining breasts. Cover the breasts with plastic wrap and refrigerate 2 hours.

3. On wax paper, mix together the cornmeal, chili powder, and cumin. Place the flour on another sheet of wax paper. In a shallow bowl, beat the egg well.

4. Roll each chicken pillow in flour. Dip in the beaten egg and dredge in cornmeal to coat completely. Place on a wire rack set over a baking sheet. Cover and refrigerate until well chilled, 2 hours or longer.

5. Place the shortening in small pieces in a deep fryer and melt, following the manufacturer's directions, or pour in 1½ inches of oil. Heat to 340°F. Fry 2 chicken pillows at a time 8 minutes, or until golden brown (to an internal temperature of 180°F.), turning once. Remove with tongs. Drain on paper towels. Keep warm while frying the remaining pieces. Remove the wooden toothpicks before serving. Serve with Tomato-Avocado Salsa.

Tomato-Avocado Salsa

1 cup finely diced seeded tomato
1 cup finely diced ripe avocado
¼ cup chopped scallions

2 tablespoons chopped fresh cilantro
2 tablespoons fresh lime juice
1 garlic clove, crushed through a press

In a medium bowl, combine all the ingredients. Stir to mix well. Cover and let stand at room temperature 30 minutes before serving.

Chinese Lemon Chicken

There are as many versions of this popular chicken dish as there are Chinese restaurants. This is one of my favorites.

Oil for frying
½ cup plus 2 tablespoons cornstarch
1 teaspoon salt
¼ teaspoon white pepper
¼ teaspoon baking soda
2 egg yolks
4 skinless, boneless chicken breast
    halves (about 5 ounces each)

3 tablespoons sugar
1 tablespoon minced fresh ginger
1 cup chicken broth
⅓ cup fresh lemon juice
¼ teaspoon grated lemon zest
2 tablespoons thinly sliced scallion
    greens

1. Pour 1 inch of oil into a deep fryer. Heat to 375°F.

2. In a pie plate, whisk together the ½ cup cornstarch, salt, pepper, baking soda, egg yolks, and ¼ cup of water until smooth. Add the chicken breasts and turn to coat thoroughly. Using tongs, lift out the chicken breasts, 1 at a time, and place in the hot oil. Fry 1 or 2 pieces at a time, turning once, until golden and crisp, 5 to 7 minutes. Drain on paper towels. Keep warm while frying the remaining chicken.

3. Meanwhile, in a medium saucepan, combine the remaining 2 tablespoons cornstarch with the sugar and ginger. Gradually stir in the chicken broth until smooth. Cook over medium-low heat, stirring constantly, until the sauce boils and thickens; boil 1 minute. Remove from the heat. Stir in the lemon juice and zest.

4. When all the chicken is fried, cut each breast crosswise on a diagonal into 4 pieces. Arrange, overlapping slightly, on a platter. Spoon enough of the sauce over the chicken to moisten lightly. Sprinkle the scallions on top. Pass the remaining sauce at the table.

Chicken Kiev

The trick here is to be sure the chicken rolls are really cold before frying, so that the frozen butter inside doesn't ooze out. Do not cut short the 1-hour freezing time for the herbed butter or the 2-hour chilling time for the chicken rolls. I like to serve Chicken Kiev with kasha mixed with small bow-tie pasta and lots of diced browned onions or with rice.

MAKES 6 SERVINGS

6 tablespoons butter, softened
2 tablespoons finely chopped fresh
    parsley
1 tablespoon minced fresh chives
1 garlic clove, crushed through a press
¼ teaspoon salt
⅛ teaspoon freshly cracked black
    pepper

6 large skinless, boneless chicken
    breast halves (7½ to 8 ounces
    each)
½ cup all-purpose flour
1¼ cups unseasoned dry bread crumbs
2 eggs
Solid vegetable shortening or oil for
    frying

1. In a small bowl, combine the butter, parsley, chives, garlic, salt, and pepper. Mash with a wooden spoon until well blended. Shape into a 6-inch square on a sheet of aluminum foil. Wrap and freeze 1 hour.

2. Remove the tenderloins from the chicken breasts and reserve for another use. Trim off any excess fat. Place each chicken half, smooth-side up, between 2 sheets of wax paper and pound with a mallet or the flat side of a cleaver to an even ¼-inch thickness, being careful not to tear the chicken. Turn over so the rough side is up.

3. Cut the butter in half, then cut it crosswise in thirds to make 6 pats. Place 1 pat of the herbed butter in the center of each chicken breast. Bring one long end up over the butter, fold in the sides, and roll up tightly, making sure no butter is showing; fasten with wooden toothpicks. You should have a 4 × 2-inch bundle. Repeat with the remaining breasts.

4. Place the flour and bread crumbs on separate sheets of wax paper. In a pie plate, beat the eggs thoroughly.

5. Dredge the chicken rolls in flour. Dip into the beaten eggs and roll in the bread crumbs to coat all over. Place on a baking sheet. Cover with plastic wrap and refrigerate at least 2 hours.

6. Place the shortening in small pieces in a deep fryer and melt, following the manufacturer's directions, or pour in 1½ inches of oil. Heat to 340°F. Fry 2 or 3 chicken bundles at a time 10 minutes, or until golden brown (to an internal temperature of 180°F.), turning once. Remove with tongs. Drain on paper towels. Keep warm while frying the remaining pieces. Remove the wooden toothpicks before serving.

Coconut Chicken Fingers

Strips of chicken marinated in lime juice and curry, coated with batter, and rolled in coconut before being fried to a crisp can be served as a main course or as an appetizer. Unsweetened shredded coconut can be found in health food stores or in the health food sections of many supermarkets.

MAKES 18 PIECES; 4 TO 5 SERVINGS

1 pound skinless, boneless chicken breast halves

¼ cup fresh lime or lemon juice

1½ teaspoons hot curry powder, such as Madras

1 teaspoon salt

¼ teaspoon ground ginger

1 cup all-purpose flour

1 teaspoon baking powder

¾ cup milk

Solid vegetable shortening or oil for frying

7 ounces shredded unsweetened coconut

Mango chutney, Peanut Sauce (page 25), or Apricot Dipping Sauce (page 39)

1. Trim all visible fat from the chicken. Cut each breast half crosswise into 6 pieces. In a medium bowl, combine the lime juice, curry powder, salt, and ground ginger. Add the chicken pieces and toss to coat. Let stand 30 minutes at room temperature.
2. In a medium bowl, whisk together the flour, baking powder, and milk until smooth. The batter will be thick. If it seems too thick, gradually thin it out with 1 to 2 tablespoons of additional milk.
3. Place the shortening in small pieces in a deep fryer and melt, following the manufacturer's directions, or pour in 1½ inches of oil. Heat to 375°F.

4. Place the coconut on a sheet of wax paper. Add the chicken pieces with the marinade to the batter and toss to coat thoroughly.

5. Using tongs, lift the chicken pieces, 1 at a time, from the batter; let excess batter drip back into the bowl. Slide the chicken into the hot oil. Fry 3 or 4 pieces at a time 2 to 3 minutes, or until golden outside and white in the center. Drain on paper towels. Serve hot or warm, with mango chutney, Peanut Sauce, or Apricot Dipping Sauce.

Fried Chicken with Biscuits and Cream Gravy

Here the chicken is poached first to make it juicier. The rosemary-flavored biscuits are fried, too!

MAKES 4 SERVINGS

1 (3-pound) broiler-fryer chicken, cut up, with breasts halved
½ cup all-purpose flour
1½ teaspoons salt
¼ teaspoon pepper

Solid vegetable shortening or oil for frying
Rosemary Biscuits (recipe follows)
¾ cup chicken broth
¾ cup heavy cream or milk

1. Place the chicken pieces in a large skillet. Cover with cold water. Bring to a boil over medium heat; reduce the heat to low. Cover and simmer 15 minutes. Drain and pat the chicken dry with paper towels.

2. In a large plastic food storage bag, mix the flour, 1 teaspoon salt, and the pepper. Add the chicken pieces a few at a time and shake to coat. When all the chicken pieces have been coated with seasoned flour, repeat to coat them again. Place on a wire rack set over a baking sheet. Let stand at room temperature 30 minutes to set the coating. Reserve 2 tablespoons of the seasoned flour left in the bag. If there is not enough, add more flour.

3. Place the shortening in small pieces in a deep fryer and melt, following the manufacturer's directions, or pour in 1½ inches of oil. Heat to 360°F. Fry the chicken pieces in batches without crowding until golden brown, 4 to 6 minutes. Drain on paper towels. (When frying the last batch of chicken, prepare the biscuit dough as described in the recipe that follows.)

4. Raise the temperature of the deep fryer to 375°F. Fry 3 or 4 biscuits at a time until golden brown, about 4 minutes, or until cooked through; test one by cutting it open. Drain on paper towels. Keep warm.

5. Remove some of the hot melted shortening or oil from the deep fryer with a metal ladle. Measure out 2 tablespoons and place in a medium saucepan. Add the reserved 2 tablespoons seasoned flour and the remaining ½ teaspoon salt. Cook, stirring, until smooth and bubbly. Gradually stir in the chicken broth, then the cream or milk. Cook over medium-low heat, stirring, until the sauce is slightly thickened and bubbly; cook 1 minute longer. Pour into a gravy boat. Serve alongside the chicken and biscuits to pour over everything.

Rosemary Biscuits

MAKES 8 TO 10 BISCUITS

1½ cups all-purpose flour

1½ teaspoons baking powder

1 teaspoon salt

2 teaspoons finely chopped fresh rosemary or ¾ teaspoon dried crumbled

¼ cup solid vegetable shortening

⅓ to ½ cup milk

In a medium bowl, combine the flour, baking powder, and salt. Mix with a fork. Stir in the rosemary. Cut in the shortening with a pastry blender until the mixture is crumbly. Stir in just enough of the milk to make a soft but not wet or sticky dough. Turn out onto a lightly floured surface. Pat to an even ½-inch thickness. Cut out biscuits with a floured 2-inch round cutter. Gather together the scraps, reroll, and cut out more biscuits.

Spicy Fried Chicken

MAKES 4 SERVINGS

2 cups buttermilk

1 tablespoon jalapeño Tabasco sauce

1¾ teaspoons ground cumin

2 teaspoons salt

2 teaspoons pepper

1 teaspoon cayenne

1 (3-pound) broiler-fryer chicken, cut up, with breasts halved

1½ cups all-purpose flour

Solid vegetable shortening or oil for frying

Chopped cilantro and lime wedges

1. In a 4-cup glass measure, combine the buttermilk, jalapeño Tabasco sauce, 1¼ teaspoons cumin, ½ teaspoon salt, ½ teaspoon pepper, and ½ teaspoon cayenne. Whisk to blend.

2. Place the chicken pieces in a sealable plastic food storage bag. Pour in the spiced buttermilk. Squeeze the bag to remove as much air as possible; seal securely. Place the bag in a large bowl and refrigerate the chicken at least 8 hours, preferably overnight.

3. In a large bowl, mix the flour with the remaining ½ teaspoon cumin, 1½ teaspoons salt, 1½ teaspoons pepper, and ½ teaspoon cayenne. Lift the chicken pieces, 1 at a time, from the buttermilk mixture and dredge in the seasoned flour; shake off any excess. When all the chicken pieces have been floured, coat the chicken a second time in the remaining flour. Place on a wire rack set over a baking sheet. Let stand at room temperature 30 minutes to set the coating.

4. Place the shortening in small pieces in a deep fryer and melt, following the manufacturer's directions, or pour in 1½ inches of oil. Heat to 340°F. Fry the chicken 2 or 3 pieces at a time, until golden brown: breasts, wings, and thighs will take 10 to 12 minutes; drumsticks will take 8 to 10 minutes (to an internal temperature of 180°F.). Drain on paper towels. Keep warm while frying the remaining chicken. Serve hot or warm, sprinkled with chopped cilantro and garnished with lime wedges to squeeze over the chicken.

Cornmeal Fried Chicken

MAKES 4 SERVINGS

1 (3-pound) broiler-fryer chicken, cut up, with breasts halved

Solid vegetable shortening or oil for frying

⅔ cup all-purpose flour

⅓ cup yellow cornmeal

¼ cup grated fresh Parmesan cheese

2 tablespoons minced fresh parsley

1 (0.7-ounce) packet Italian salad dressing mix

½ teaspoon baking powder

¼ teaspoon garlic powder

⅔ cup milk

2 tablespoons vegetable oil

1 egg

1. Place the chicken pieces in a large skillet. Cover with lightly salted water. Bring to a boil over medium heat; reduce the heat to low, cover, and simmer for 20 minutes. Drain the chicken and pat dry with paper towels. Remove the skin if you wish.

2. Place the shortening in small pieces in a deep fryer and melt, following the manufacturer's directions, or pour in 1½ inches of oil. Heat to 360°F.

3. In a medium bowl, mix together the flour, cornmeal, Parmesan cheese, parsley, salad dressing mix, baking powder, and garlic powder.

4. Pour the milk into a 2-cup glass measure. Add the 2 tablespoons oil and the egg; beat well to combine. Add to the seasoned cornmeal and beat until the batter is smooth.

5. Dip the chicken pieces, 1 at a time, in the batter; let any excess batter drip back into the bowl. Fry the chicken in batches without crowding, turning once, until golden, about 3 minutes. Drain on paper towels. Keep warm while frying the remaining chicken pieces. Serve hot.

Beer-Batter Fried Chicken

This is a family recipe that I have used throughout the years. I hope you like it as much as we do.

MAKES 4 SERVINGS

1⅔ cups all-purpose flour
1½ teaspoons garlic powder
1½ teaspoons salt
1⅛ teaspoons pepper
1 teaspoon paprika
¼ teaspoon poultry seasoning

1 egg yolk
¾ cup flat beer
1 (3-pound) broiler-fryer chicken, cut
   up, with breasts halved
Solid vegetable shortening or oil for
   frying

1. In a large bowl, combine 1 cup of the flour, the garlic powder, 1 teaspoon salt, 1 teaspoon pepper, the paprika, and the poultry seasoning. Mix with a fork.

2. In a medium bowl, combine the remaining ⅔ cup flour, ½ teaspoon salt, and ⅛ teaspoon pepper. In a small bowl, beat the egg yolk into the beer until well blended. Whisk into the flour mixture in the medium bowl until the batter is smooth. The batter will be thick.

3. Moisten the chicken pieces lightly with water. Coat the chicken pieces, 1 at a time, in the seasoned flour; then dip into the batter, letting the excess drip back into the bowl or use your fingers to coat the chicken with the batter. Dip the chicken pieces back into the seasoned flour, coating thoroughly. Place on a wire rack set over a baking sheet. Let stand at room temperature 30 minutes to set the coating.

4. Place the shortening in small pieces in a deep fryer and melt, following the manufacturer's directions, or pour in 1½ inches of oil. Heat to 360°F. Fry the chicken in batches, a few pieces at a time, until golden brown: breast halves, wings, and thighs will take 10 to 12 minutes; drumsticks will take 8 to 10 minutes (to an internal temperature of 180°F.). Drain on paper towels. Serve hot or at room temperature.

Chinese-Style Fried Chicken with Broccoli

This batter-coated, double-fried chicken can be partially prepared a few hours in advance, but the final cooking should take place just before serving. For efficiency, have all the ingredients measured out on a tray ready to go. Serve over steamed white rice.

MAKES 6 SERVINGS

1 pound skinless, boneless chicken thighs or chicken breasts
Oil for frying
½ cup all-purpose flour
5 tablespoons cornstarch
½ teaspoon baking powder
1 egg
3 tablespoons hoisin sauce
2 tablespoons soy sauce
1½ tablespoons rice wine, sake, or dry white wine

1 tablespoon sugar
3 cups broccoli florets (8 ounces)
2 garlic cloves, smashed
6 small dried hot red peppers, stems and seeds removed
2 quarter-size slices of peeled fresh ginger
1 cup (1-inch) scallion pieces

1. Trim as much visible fat from the chicken as possible; cut into approximately 2-inch cubes.

2. Pour 1½ inches of oil into a deep fryer. Heat to 375°F.

3. In a medium bowl, combine the flour, ¼ cup cornstarch, and the baking powder. In a 1-cup glass measure, beat the egg. Beat in enough water to equal ½ cup liquid. Whisk into the cornstarch mixture until smooth. If the batter seems to be too thick, add 1 to 2 tablespoons of water to thin out slightly. Add the chicken pieces and toss to coat with the batter.

4. Lift the chicken pieces a few at a time from the batter; let any excess drip back into the bowl. Place 5 chicken pieces in the hot fat. Fry 3 minutes, or until pale golden but not brown. Drain on paper towels. Repeat with the remaining chicken pieces. (The dish can be prepared to this point and refrigerated for up to 2 hours, until ready to use.)

5. In a small bowl, combine the hoisin sauce, soy sauce, rice wine, sugar, and the remaining 1 tablespoon cornstarch. Whisk in ½ cup of water until smooth.

6. Reheat the oil in the deep fryer to 375°F. Place 5 pieces of the precooked chicken in the hot fat. Fry until golden brown, about 3 minutes. Drain on paper towels. Repeat with the remaining chicken pieces. Remove some of the hot fat from the deep fryer with a metal ladle. Measure out 2 tablespoons and place in a heatproof cup.

7. In a wok or large skillet, heat 1 tablespoon of the oil over high heat. Add the broccoli and toss to coat with the oil. Add ¼ cup of water, cover, and steam 3 minutes, or just until the broccoli turns bright green. Drain and place in a bowl.

8. Heat the remaining 1 tablespoon oil in the wok. Add the garlic, dried hot peppers, ginger, and the scallions. Stir-fry over medium heat until the garlic begins to brown. Remove and discard the garlic and ginger.

9. Pour the hoisin sauce mixture into the skillet. Cook over medium heat, stirring, until the sauce thickens, about 1 minute. Add the chicken and the broccoli; stir lightly to coat with the sauce. Serve at once.

Sizzling Meats

Variety is guaranteed when you use the deep fryer to prepare this sizzling selection of popular meat favorites. Beef, pork, veal, and lamb fry up crisp and succulent in a matter of minutes.

I was surprised to discover how easily lean meats cook in a deep fryer. Often they don't even need turning. And because you are frying at a high temperature, very little oil—at most, no more than 1 tablespoon—is absorbed.

The array of recipes that follows borrows from several ethnic cuisines—Chinese, Mexican, Middle Eastern, and American. You can choose from Chicken-Fried Steak with Gravy, a Southern favorite, Ham Croquettes with Cheese Sauce, or Lamb Meatballs in Curried Yogurt Sauce. Want Chinese? Try Szechuan Beef and Scallions, or, for Mexican fare, Beef and Bean Chimichangas. Kids and grown-ups alike will love Corn Dawgs, frankfurters encased in a cornmeal batter.

Many of the recipes are completely cooked in the deep fryer while others need the additional boost of top-of-the-stove cooking or oven baking.

Hints and Tips

- Meat should be thoroughly dried before coating with crumbs or dipping in batter.
- Meats should be cut the same size or thickness to allow for even frying.
- Use large eggs in the recipes that call for eggs.

Corn Dawgs

Popular in the South, these batter-coated frankfurters can be found at many outdoor festivals and country fairs, and they are great favorites with the kids. Beef, chicken, or turkey frankfurters work equally well. I found that placing the batter in a tall glass makes for easier dipping. For these you'll need 8 to 10 wooden craft sticks or round wooden skewers. You can find the flat wooden craft sticks at any craft store.

MAKES 4 TO 5 SERVINGS OF 2 FRANKFURTERS EACH

Oil for frying
1 (16-ounce) package frankfurters
   (8 to 10)
¾ cup all-purpose flour
⅔ cup yellow cornmeal
2 tablespoons sugar
1½ teaspoons baking powder

¼ teaspoon salt
¾ cup plus 1 tablespoon milk
1 egg
1 tablespoon minced onion
Mustard, ketchup, relish, and chopped
   onion

1. Pour 1 inch of oil into a deep fryer. Heat to 375°F.

2. Pat the frankfurters dry with paper towels. Insert a wooden stick into 1 end of each frankfurter, leaving about 1½ inches exposed for a handle.

3. In a large bowl, combine the flour, cornmeal, sugar, baking powder, and salt. Stir with a fork or whisk gently to blend. In a small bowl, whisk together ¾ cup of the milk with the egg and onion. Add to the cornmeal mixture and whisk until smooth. If the batter seems thick, add the additional 1 tablespoon milk. Pour the batter into a tall glass.

4. Dip 1 frankfurter at a time into the batter in the glass and twirl to coat; let any excess batter drip back into the glass. Lower 2 or 3 dipped frankfurters at a time into the hot oil. Fry, turning once, 2 to 3 minutes, until golden. Remove with tongs and drain on paper towels. If the batter becomes too thick, add more milk, 1 teaspoon at a time. You will have to tilt the glass to coat the last few frankfurters. To eat, dip into mustard or ketchup, then into relish or onion.

SAFETY NOTE: Round wooden skewers have a point at one end. For children under 6, cut off the point; caution older children.

Szechuan Beef and Scallions

No need to order in Chinese takeout when you can make authentic-tasting dishes like this so easily. This very savory beef dish is quick to prepare. The meat is first deep-fried; then the dish is finished on top of the stove in a wok or skillet. Freezing the meat for a few hours makes for easier slicing. Serve with steamed white rice.

MAKES 4 SERVINGS

1 pound beef flank steak
¼ cup bottled chili sauce
2 tablespoons reduced-sodium soy
    sauce
1 tablespoon dry sherry
1 teaspoon cornstarch
1½ teaspoons grated fresh ginger

¼ teaspoon crushed hot pepper flakes
Peanut or other oil for frying
3 garlic cloves, crushed through a
    press
4 scallions, cut on the diagonal into
    1-inch pieces

1. Place the beef on a baking sheet and freeze 1 hour or longer, until firm but not frozen hard. Trim off any visible fat. Cut the meat lengthwise in half then cut crosswise on an angle into very thin (⅛-inch) slices.

2. In a small bowl, combine the chili sauce, soy sauce, sherry, cornstarch, ginger, and hot pepper. Stir to blend the cornstarch.

3. Pour 1 inch of oil into a deep fryer. Heat to 365°F. Fry the beef in several batches 30 to 45 seconds, or until browned around the edges. Drain on paper towels. Remove a little of the oil from the fryer with a metal ladle and measure out 1 tablespoon with a metal spoon.

4. In a wok or large skillet, heat the reserved 1 tablespoon oil from the beef over medium-high heat. Add the garlic and scallions and stir-fry 1 minute. Add the chili sauce and the cooked meat; toss to combine. Stir-fry until the sauce thickens and becomes bubbly and coats the meat, about 1 minute. Serve at once.

Philadelphia Cheese Steak Sandwiches

The origin of this beef and cheese sandwich served on a hoagie-type roll has never been authenticated, although it is a specialty of Philadelphia. An order for "cheese with" means the dish should come with sautéed onions.

MAKES 4 SANDWICHES

4 (3-ounce) beef bracciole (thin-sliced lean beef round steak)
Meat tenderizer
4 tablespoons butter
4 medium onions, sliced

Oil for frying
¼ teaspoon pepper
4 (7-inch-long) soft hoagie rolls
8 ounces coarsely shredded sharp Cheddar, Colby, or American cheese

1. Moisten the meat lightly with a dampened paper towel. Sprinkle meat tenderizer over both sides, using about ½ teaspoon per pound, or follow the manufacturer's directions for usage. Cut each bracciole crosswise in half, then pound each side with a meat mallet to a ⅛-inch thickness.

2. In a large skillet, melt the butter over medium heat. Add the onions and toss to coat. Cook over medium-low heat, stirring occasionally, until softened and slightly golden, 12 to 15 minutes. Remove from the heat and cover to keep warm.

3. Preheat the broiler. Pour ¾ inch of oil into a deep fryer. Heat to 375°F. Add the meat in batches of 2 or 3 pieces and fry 1 minute, or until the meat is lightly browned. Drain on paper towels. When all the meat is fried, season with the pepper.

4. Cut the rolls lengthwise in half. Arrange the bottom halves, cut-side up, on a large baking sheet. Top each with 2 pieces of meat, ¼ cup onions, and ½ cup shredded cheese. Place the tops of the rolls, cut-side up, on the baking sheet. Place under the broiler 15 seconds, just until the cheese melts. (Watch carefully so the tops of the rolls do not burn.) Sandwich together and serve at once.

Sweet and Pungent Pork

Pineapple chunks and juice provide the sweet, and mixed sweet pickles and their juice provide the pungent in this popular Chinese recipe. The addition of plum tomato strips and snow peas makes for a colorful and very flavorful dish. Serve hot over white or brown rice.

MAKES 6 SERVINGS

3 center-cut boneless pork chops, cut 1 inch thick (1 pound)

2 teaspoons dry sherry

1 tablespoon cornstarch

½ teaspoon salt

2 ounces trimmed snow peas

Peanut or other oil for frying

2 or 3 garlic cloves, crushed through a press

1 (8-ounce) can pineapple chunks with their juices, drained, with juices reserved

¼ cup sweet mixed pickles, with ¼ cup of their juices

2 tablespoons reduced-sodium soy sauce

2 large plum tomatoes, cut into 6 thin wedges each

1. Trim any visible fat from the pork. Cut the meat into 1-inch cubes. Place the pork in a medium bowl. Add the sherry, 1 teaspoon of the cornstarch, and the salt; toss to coat. Let stand 15 minutes.

2. Meanwhile, drop the snow peas into a medium saucepan of boiling water. As soon as the water returns to a boil, drain the snow peas and rinse under cold running water. Drain well and pat dry.

3. Pour 1 inch of oil into a deep fryer. Heat to 365°F. Place enough of the pork cubes in the dryer basket to cover the bottom in a single layer without touching. Slowly lower the basket into the hot oil. The oil will bubble up, so be careful. Fry 5

to 6 minutes, until the pork is done: white in the center and slightly browned on the outside. Drain on paper towels. If any of the pork sticks to the wire basket, use a wooden spoon to release. Repeat with the remaining pork cubes. Remove a little of the oil from the deep fryer with a metal ladle. Measure out 1 tablespoon.

4. In a wok or large skillet, heat the reserved 1 tablespoon oil over medium-high heat. Add the garlic and stir-fry 30 seconds. Add the pineapple juice, sweet pickle juice, and soy sauce. Bring to a boil. Add the pineapple chunks, sweet mixed pickles, snow peas, and browned pork; stir to combine.

5. In a small cup, combine the remaining 2 teaspoons cornstarch with 1 tablespoon water. Mix well. Stir into the wok. Cook, stirring, until the sauce thickens and coats the meat and vegetables, 1 to 2 minutes. Stir in the tomatoes and serve at once.

Double-Crust Sausage Pizzas

These rustic-looking two-crust pizzas, filled with savory sausage and cheese, are generous and very hearty. Serve with a tossed green salad.

MAKES 8 SERVINGS

3½ cups all-purpose flour
1 (¼-ounce) envelope active dry yeast
1 teaspoon salt
1 cup hot water (125° to 130°F.)
½ cup vegetable oil, plus oil for frying
½ pound sweet turkey or Italian pork
   sausage, casings removed

½ cup jarred natural pizza sauce
   (without sugar)
¼ teaspoon dried oregano
¼ teaspoon dried basil
1 cup coarsely shredded mozzarella
   cheese
2 tablespoons grated Parmesan cheese

1. In a large bowl, combine 1½ cups of the flour with the yeast and salt. Stir with a fork to mix. In a 2-cup glass measure, stir together the hot water with the ½ cup oil. Blend into the yeast mixture. Stir in another 1½ cups flour to make a soft dough. Not all of the flour will be absorbed.

2. Spread the remaining ½ cup flour on a flat work surface. Turn out the dough onto the flour and knead 5 to 7 minutes, or until the dough is smooth and no longer sticky, working in the remaining flour as you knead.

3. Place the dough in a lightly greased bowl. Turn to bring the greased side up. Cover with plastic wrap and let rise away from drafts until doubled in volume, about 45 minutes.

4. Meanwhile, crumble the sausage into a large nonstick skillet. Cook over medium heat, breaking up large pieces with a wooden spoon, until the meat is lightly browned and no longer pink, 8 to 10 minutes. Remove from the heat and drain off any excess fat.

5. Punch down the dough in the bowl. Turn out onto the work surface and shape into a ball. Cover with the bowl and let rest 10 minutes. Divide the dough into 8 equal pieces; shape each into a ball. Working with 1 piece at a time, roll out into a 6-inch round (keep the remaining dough covered to prevent drying out).

6. In a small bowl, stir together the pizza sauce, oregano, and basil. Spread 1 tablespoon of this sauce over each circle to within ½ inch of the edge. Sprinkle about 1½ tablespoons of the sausage, 2 tablespoons of the mozzarella, and ¾ teaspoon of the Parmesan cheese. Bring one edge of the dough over the filling and press to seal securely, using the side of your thumb. Press the edges on both sides with the floured tines of a fork. Trim the edges to even them with a pastry cutter or small knife. As you finish each pizza, lift it onto a large baking sheet with a pancake turner. Place in the refrigerator while heating the oil.

7. Pour ¾ to 1 inch of oil into a deep fryer. Heat to 375°F. Carefully slide 1 pizza into the hot oil with a wide slotted metal spatula. Fry 5 to 6 minutes, until golden, turning once. Drain on paper towels. Serve hot.

NOTE: Fried pizzas can be frozen. To reheat: Place on brown paper-lined baking sheets. Bake the frozen pizzas in a preheated 425°F. oven 15 to 20 minutes, or until hot.

Scotch Eggs

Prepare the hard-cooked eggs the night before, so they are very cold when they are encased with the sausage; otherwise the sausage will slip off the eggs.

MAKES 6 SERVINGS

1 pound sweet turkey sausage, casings removed

2 tablespoons finely chopped fresh parsley

1 teaspoon fennel seeds, slightly crushed

½ teaspoon salt

¼ teaspoon white pepper

6 hard-cooked eggs, shelled and well chilled

2 raw eggs

⅓ to ½ cup unseasoned dry bread crumbs

3 tablespoons all-purpose flour

Oil for frying

1. In a medium bowl, combine the sausage, parsley, fennel seeds, salt, white pepper, and 2 tablespoons water. Mix lightly with a fork until blended. Divide into 6 equal portions, about ⅓ cup each.

2. With slightly dampened hands, press 1 portion of the meat mixture around each hard-cooked egg, completely enclosing the egg.

3. In a pie plate, beat the raw eggs until frothy. Place the bread crumbs on a sheet of wax paper. Place the sausage-covered eggs on a separate sheet of wax paper. Sift the flour over the eggs through a small fine-mesh sieve, turning the eggs to coat completely with flour. Dip each sausage-coated egg into the beaten eggs, then roll in the bread crumbs to coat completely (use the edges of the wax paper to aid in rolling). Shape into an oval like an egg. Place on a baking sheet and refrigerate while the oil heats.

4. Pour 1 inch of oil into a deep fryer. Heat to 350°F. Fry in batches, 3 at a time, 5 to 6 minutes, until golden, turning once. Drain on paper towels. Serve hot or cold.

Beef and Bean Chimichangas

½ pound lean ground beef or turkey
1 medium onion, chopped
2 garlic cloves, crushed through a
   press
1 (15-ounce) can red kidney or pinto
   beans, drained
1 (8-ounce) can tomato sauce

1 tablespoon chili powder
½ teaspoon salt
12 burrito-size flour tortillas (8 inches
   in diameter)
1 cup coarsely shredded Monterey Jack
   cheese with jalapeño peppers
Oil for frying

1. In a large nonstick skillet, cook the meat, onion, and garlic over medium heat, stirring to break up the lumps, until the meat has browned, the onion has softened, and the liquid has evaporated, about 10 minutes. Drain off any fat.

2. Add the beans, tomato sauce, chili powder, and salt to the skillet. Simmer over low heat, stirring frequently, about 10 minutes.

3. Preheat the oven to 350°F. Place the tortillas in a clean moistened kitchen towel and wrap in aluminum foil. Heat in the oven 10 minutes. Or place the tortillas between moistened paper towels on a plate. Microwave on medium 1 to 1½ minutes.

4. Forming 1 at a time, scoop ¼ cup meat filling into the center of a warm tortilla. Sprinkle with 2½ tablespoons of the cheese. Bring the bottom edge of the tortilla up over the filling, fold in the sides, and roll up. Secure with wooden toothpicks.

5. Pour 1 inch of oil into a deep fryer. Heat to 375°F. Fry the chimichangas, 2 at a time, for 2 minutes, or until golden, turning once. Remove with tongs. Drain on paper towels. Serve hot. Remove the toothpicks before serving.

Fresh Tomato Salsa

Salsa is a general term for seasoned sauces, which are used either for dipping or as a topping. During the summer months, orange tomatoes, the color of choice here, are plentiful in farmers' markets. Feel free to substitute yellow or red.

MAKES 1⅓ CUPS

¾ pound ripe orange, yellow, or red tomatoes (2 to 3 medium)
¼ cup finely chopped onion
2 garlic cloves, crushed through a press
1 tablespoon corn or other vegetable oil

2 to 3 teaspoons minced seeded jalapeño pepper, to taste
1 teaspoon salt
1½ tablespoons chopped fresh cilantro

1. Plunge the tomatoes into a saucepan of boiling water for 1 minute; immediately remove to a bowl of ice and water. Peel off the skins with a small, sharp knife; they will slip off easily. Coarsely chop the tomatoes, but do not seed them.

2. In a medium saucepan, cook the onion and garlic in the oil over medium heat until soft, about 2 minutes. Add the tomatoes and jalapeño pepper. Cook over medium-low heat, stirring occasionally, 10 minutes. Stir in the salt and cilantro.

3. Pour into a food processor and puree until smooth. Pour into a small bowl. Serve warm or at room temperature.

Tomatillo Salsa

A tomatillo resembles a small green tomato surrounded with a papery husk. Actually it is not a tomato at all, but rather a berry from the family Physalis. You can find them in the produce section of most supermarkets, at specialty food stores and farmers' markets. Tomatillos are also available canned.

MAKES 1½ CUPS

¾ pound tomatillos
¼ cup chopped scallions
2 garlic cloves, crushed through a
   press
¼ cup chopped fresh cilantro

2 to 3 teaspoons chopped seeded
   jalapeño pepper, to taste
1 teaspoon salt
3 to 4 tablespoons water

Husk, rinse, and quarter the tomatillos. Place in a food processor with the scallions, garlic, cilantro, jalapeño pepper, and salt. Puree until smooth. Pour into a small bowl. If necessary, add water, 1 tablespoon at a time, until the salsa is the desired dip consistency. If made ahead, cover and refrigerate. Serve at room temperature.

Chicken-Fried Steak with Gravy

Of course, there's no chicken here, just a cooking technique that's similar to that of Southern fried chicken. It's a way of transforming a less tender cut of beef into a tempting plate of food. The gravy is made with either milk or cream. The traditional accompaniment is mashed potatoes, to enjoy with all the extra gravy.

MAKES 4 SERVINGS

1 cup all-purpose flour
1 teaspoon salt
½ teaspoon pepper
½ teaspoon hot Hungarian paprika or
  ½ teaspoon paprika and
  ⅛ teaspoon cayenne

1 pound beef top round steak, cut
  ½ inch thick
1 egg
Oil for frying
2 cups milk or light cream

1. In a small bowl, combine the flour, salt, pepper, and paprika. Mix well. Remove ¼ cup of the seasoned flour and set aside for gravy.

2. Trim any visible fat from the meat and cut into 4 equal pieces. Sprinkle both sides of each piece of meat with 1 tablespoon of the seasoned flour. Pound the meat with a mallet until it is an even ⅛ inch thick.

3. In a pie plate, beat the egg with 2 tablespoons of water until blended. Place the remaining ½ cup seasoned flour on wax paper. Dredge the meat in the flour, then dip in the egg and back into the flour to coat completely. Set on a wire rack.

4. Pour 1 inch of oil into a deep fryer. Heat to 375°F. Fry 2 pieces of meat at a time until golden, about 2 minutes. Drain on paper towels. Keep warm.

5. When all the steak is fried, place the reserved ¼ cup seasoned flour in a large skillet. Gradually whisk in the milk until smooth. Cook over medium-low heat, stirring constantly, until the gravy comes to a boil and thickens, about 3 minutes. Arrange the meat on a platter. Spoon some gravy over the meat and pass the remainder on the side.

Wiener Schnitzel

Wiener means "Viennese," but this recipe is usually attributed to German cooking. Bread the meat just before you are ready to fry. To make Holstein Schnitzel, omit the anchovies and lemon and top each serving with a fried egg.

MAKES 4 SERVINGS

1 pound veal scallops or turkey cutlets
½ teaspoon salt
¼ teaspoon pepper
2 eggs
¼ teaspoon grated lemon zest

3 tablespoons all-purpose flour
½ cup dry bread crumbs
Oil for frying
Lemon slices, rolled anchovies, and dill
   or parsley sprigs, as garnish

1. Pound the meat with the flat side of a mallet until thin as for scaloppine. Sprinkle the meat with the salt and pepper. In a pie plate, beat the eggs with the lemon zest until foamy. On separate sheets of wax paper, place the flour and the bread crumbs.
2. Dredge the meat in the flour, shaking off any excess. Dip the meat into the eggs; let the excess drip back into the plate. Coat the meat thoroughly with bread crumbs. Place on a wire rack to dry.
3. Pour 1 inch of oil into a deep fryer. Heat to 375°F. Fry the cutlets, 1 or 2 at a time (do not crowd), until golden, about 30 to 45 seconds, turning once. Drain on paper towels. Keep warm while frying the remaining cutlets. Overlap the cutlets on a serving platter. Top the meat with lemon slices and rolled anchovies. Garnish with dill or parsley sprigs.

Ham Croquettes with Cheese Sauce

The word croquette *is French in origin, from* croquer, *"to crunch," which describes nicely the crisp golden brown coating that surrounds any croquette. This preparation is an excellent way to use up leftover meats and vegetables. The croquettes can be shaped into little cones or tapered ovals. For easier handling and shaping, the mixture must be well chilled. Cooked chicken or turkey can be substituted for the ham suggested here.*

MAKES 4 SERVINGS

---

2 tablespoons finely chopped green bell
    pepper
2 tablespoons finely chopped scallions
3 tablespoons butter
⅓ cup plus ¼ cup all-purpose flour
1 cup milk
2½ cups finely ground or minced
    cooked ham

1 tablespoon minced fresh sage or 1
    teaspoon crumbled dried
¼ teaspoon salt
¼ teaspoon pepper
½ cup dry bread crumbs
1 egg
Oil for frying
Cheese Sauce (recipe follows)

1. In a large skillet, cook the bell pepper and scallions in the butter over medium heat, until soft, about 2 minutes. Stir in ⅓ cup of the flour. Cook 1 minute; the mixture will clump. Remove from the heat. Gradually stir in the milk until the mixture is smooth. Cook over medium-low heat, stirring constantly, until the mixture is very thick and bubbly. Remove from the heat.

2. Stir in the ham, sage, salt, and pepper. Spread the mixture evenly in the skillet; cover with plastic wrap. Refrigerate until very well chilled, preferably overnight.

3. The next day, divide the mixture into 12 even portions (about 3 level tablespoons each). Shape each into a small cone about 2 inches high and 2 inches at the base or form into a 3½-inch tapered cylinder.

4. On separate sheets of wax paper, place the remaining ¼ cup of flour and the bread crumbs. In a pie plate, beat the egg with 1 tablespoon water.

5. Gently roll each croquette in flour to coat. Dip in the egg and roll in the crumbs to coat. Place on a baking sheet. Let stand at room temperature 30 minutes, or refrigerate up to 2 hours, until ready to fry.

6. Pour 1½ inches of oil into a deep fryer. Heat to 375°F. Fry the croquettes, 3 at a time, until golden brown, 2 to 2½ minutes per batch. Drain on paper towels. To serve, place 3 croquettes on each plate. Spoon some of the cheese sauce over the croquettes. Pass the remainder at the table.

Cheese Sauce

This sauce is also good over steamed vegetables. Try it on cauliflower, topped with buttered crumbs.

MAKES 1½ CUPS

3 tablespoons butter
3 tablespoons all-purpose flour
¼ teaspoon salt

1½ cups milk
¼ cup grated fresh Parmesan cheese
1 teaspoon Dijon mustard

In a medium saucepan, melt the butter over medium heat. Whisk in the flour and salt and cook, stirring, 1 minute. Remove from the heat. Gradually whisk in the milk until the mixture is smooth. Cook over low heat, stirring constantly, until the mixture thickens and begins to bubble, about 1 minute. Stir in the cheese and mustard and serve.

Barbecued Ribs

These ribs are first fried in the deep fryer, then coated with a bottled barbecue sauce and finished up in the oven. The flavor is as good as the sauce you use. Provide plenty of paper napkins as this is messy, but, oh so good, eating. These ribs can also be served as an appetizer; allow three ribs per serving.

MAKES 2 SERVINGS

2 eggs
¼ cup cornstarch
2 tablespoons Worcestershire sauce
2 pounds meaty baby back ribs, cut
    into individual ribs and patted dry

Oil for frying
1 cup bottled thick barbecue sauce

1. In a large bowl, whisk together the eggs, cornstarch, and Worcestershire sauce until smooth. Add the ribs and toss to coat thoroughly. Let stand at room temperature for 15 minutes.

2. Pour 1½ inches of oil into a deep fryer. Heat to 300°F. Fry the ribs 3 or 4 at a time until crisp and brown, about 6 minutes. Drain on paper towels.

3. While the last batch of ribs are frying, preheat the oven to 350°F. Line a large baking sheet with aluminum foil for easier cleanup.

4. Brush the fried ribs generously with the bottled barbecue sauce. Bake in the oven 30 to 40 minutes, until ribs are tender and sauce has glazed the ribs. Turn once. Serve with additional heated barbecue sauce, if desired.

Sesame Pork with Lemon Sauce

Ginger, soy sauce, and black sesame seeds add flavor to these fried tenderloin cutlets, which are then drizzled with a flavorful citrus sauce. You can purchase black sesame seeds in Asian markets.

MAKES 4 SERVINGS

1 (1-pound) pork tenderloin
1 tablespoon dry sherry
1 tablespoon reduced-sodium soy sauce
1 teaspoon grated fresh ginger
½ teaspoon salt
1 egg

2 tablespoons cornstarch
2 tablespoons all-purpose flour
1 tablespoon black or regular sesame seeds
Oil for frying
Lemon Sauce (recipe follows)

1. Cut the pork tenderloin crosswise on an angle into slices ½ inch thick. Trim off visible fat. Pound the slices ¼ inch thick between 2 sheets of wax paper with the flat side of a mallet.

2. In a pie plate, combine the sherry, soy sauce, ginger, and salt. Coat the pork slices, 1 piece at a time, with the marinade. Let stand in the pie plate 30 minutes.

3. In a small bowl, beat the egg with 1 tablespoon of water until foamy. Pour the mixture over the pork and turn to coat the meat slices. On wax paper, combine the cornstarch, flour, and sesame seeds. Lightly dredge the pork slices on both sides. Place on a wire rack to dry.

4. Pour 1 inch of oil into a deep fryer. Heat to 350°F. Fry the pork slices, a few pieces at a time (do not crowd), until golden, 3 minutes, turning once. Drain on paper towels. Keep warm while frying the remaining meat. Spoon on the sauce and serve.

Lemon Sauce

¼ cup fresh lemon juice

¼ cup reduced-sodium soy sauce

2 tablespoons sugar

2 tablespoons dry sherry

1 teaspoon grated lemon zest

1 teaspoon grated fresh ginger

⅛ teaspoon salt

1½ teaspoons cornstarch

In a small saucepan, combine the lemon juice, soy sauce, sugar, sherry, lemon zest, ginger, and salt. Bring to a boil over medium heat, stirring frequently. In a small cup, combine the cornstarch with 1 tablespoon water. Stir into the hot mixture. Cook and stir until the mixture comes to a boil and thickens slightly, about 1 minute.

Lamb Meatballs in Curried Yogurt Sauce

This Middle Eastern dish has lots of flavor. The besan called for in the recipe is chickpea flour, available where Indian foods are sold. You can substitute all-purpose flour. Make sure you take the yogurt out of the refrigerator and keep it at room temperature until ready to use. Serve the meatballs over hot cooked rice and top with chopped cilantro, slivered almonds, and currants.

MAKES 4 SERVINGS

1 pound lean ground lamb or beef
1 egg
6 tablespoons plus 2 teaspoons
  chickpea flour (*besan)* or
  all-purpose flour
1 teaspoon salt
¼ teaspoon pepper
Oil for frying
4 tablespoons butter
1 cup minced onions

2 tablespoons minced fresh ginger
2 teaspoons minced fresh garlic
1 teaspoon ground coriander
1 teaspoon ground cumin
½ teaspoon turmeric
½ teaspoon cayenne
2 cups plain yogurt, at room
  temperature
Condiments: chopped cilantro, slivered
  almonds, currants (optional garnish)

1. In a food processor, place the meat, egg, 3 tablespoons of the chickpea flour, the salt, and pepper. Process until the meat is smooth and begins to gather around the blades. Shape the meat into 16 meatballs, about 2 level tablespoons each.

2. In a small cup, combine 3 tablespoons of the chickpea flour with ¼ cup water and mix until smooth. With your fingers or a pastry brush, coat the meatballs lightly with the batter. Place on a wire rack.

3. Pour 1½ inches of oil into a deep fryer. Heat to 375°F. Fry the meatballs, 3 or 4 at a time, until golden brown, about 5 minutes. Drain on paper towels.

4. In a large skillet over medium-low heat, melt the butter. Add the onions, ginger, and garlic. Cook and stir until golden, about 5 minutes. Add the coriander, cumin, turmeric, and cayenne; cook, stirring, 1 minute. Remove the skillet from the heat. Whisk the remaining 2 teaspoons chickpea flour into the yogurt and gradually whisk the yogurt into the saucepan until the mixture is smooth. Add the meatballs and turn to coat with the sauce. Cook over low heat, spooning the sauce over the meatballs, until heated through. Serve over hot cooked rice. Garnish with chopped cilantro, almonds, and currants.

Fish and Chips and More

The catch of the day is definitely the deep fryer. You, too, will get hooked on using this convenient appliance to create restaurant favorites, such as fried shrimp, calamari, scallops, or flounder, batter-coated fish fingers, clam fritters, or crab cakes. Whether the fish were caught or bought, these deep-fried, fast, and foolproof fish recipes will guarantee that no one in your house will say, "I don't like fish."

If you are concerned about the odor of fried fish, forget about it! All covered deep fryers have built-in or removable charcoal filters, which screen out odors. A few also have built-in timers, which is an asset when frying fish.

Fish fries fast in a deep fryer, anywhere from 1 to 4 minutes depending upon thickness, so it is important to maintain the temperature of the oil at 375°F. at all times. At this temperature, the coating will brown evenly, keeping the fish moist and juicy inside. Fry only a few pieces of fish at a time, and bring the temperature back to 375°F. before adding more fish. It is better to undercook than overcook fish. Test 1 piece for doneness. You can always add more frying time.

Crumb coatings adhere better if the coated fish is left to stand on a wire rack for 30 minutes at room temperature or refrigerated for up to 1 hour before frying. If refrigerated, remove from the refrigerator while heating the oil. Lift batter-coated fish with tongs and slide the fish into the hot oil. To remove fillets or fried cakes from the oil, use a wide, slotted metal spatula. Use the metal fryer basket when frying fritters and small seafood. Tilt the fryer basket slightly to eliminate any oil that may still be clinging to the fish before placing on paper towel-lined trays to drain.

Most oils can be used to fry fish. Peanut, olive, and corn oils give a more pronounced flavor than the milder oils, such as vegetable, canola, or blends. During frying, remove any loose bits of batter or crumbs from the oil to prevent the oil from deteriorating.

Hints and Tips

- For best results, fish fillets or fish fingers should be even in size and cut no more than ½ to ¾ inch thick.
- Buy fish from a reputable fish market. Fresh fish does not smell; it should be springy to the touch and have good color.
- If your deep fryer does not have a built-in timer, use a timer with a minute and second feature.

Fried Calamari

This is one of the simplest of recipes to prepare. Have all the ingredients assembled for frying as it goes very fast. Flour the squid just before you're ready to fry to prevent the squid from becoming gummy. Adding baking soda to the flour aids in browning and also gives the squid a crunchy bite. If you are cleaning the squid yourself, rather than having the fishmonger do it for you, you will need 2½ pounds.

MAKES 4 SERVINGS

2 pounds cleaned squid
Salt and pepper
Oil for frying

1 cup all-purpose flour
1 teaspoon baking soda
Lemon wedges and hot pepper sauce

1. Rinse the squid inside and out with cold water. Cut the squid into ¼-inch rings and cut the large tentacles in half lengthwise. Place the squid in a colander and toss with your fingers to remove excess water. Pat as dry as possible with paper towels. This is important to prevent splattering in the hot oil. Season the squid with salt and pepper to taste.

2. Pour 1½ inches of oil into a deep fryer. Heat to 375°F.

3. In a large bowl, stir together the flour and baking soda. Add one-fourth of the squid to the flour mixture and toss to coat. Lift out the squid with a slotted spoon or your fingers and transfer to a large wire-mesh strainer. Shake any excess flour back into the bowl.

4. Place the squid in the fryer basket and gently lower it into the hot oil. The oil will bubble up, so be careful. Fry 1½ to 2 minutes, or until the edges of the squid rings are lightly browned. Do not overcook, or the squid will toughen to rubber bands. Drain on paper towels. Keep warm while repeating 3 more times, with the remaining squid and flour mixture. Serve hot with lemon wedges, hot pepper sauce, and salt and pepper to taste.

Spicy Fried Shrimp

These shrimp are simply delicious and so easy to prepare. You can turn them into a salad by placing the hot shrimp over mesclun, a mixture of small baby lettuces, tossed with a light fruity olive oil and a little lemon juice and adding chunks or slices of papaya.

MAKES 4 SERVINGS

1 tablespoon olive oil

2 garlic cloves, crushed through a press

1 tablespoon finely chopped fresh cilantro

1 teaspoon finely shredded fresh ginger

½ teaspoon hot pepper flakes, slightly crushed

½ teaspoon lime zest

¼ teaspoon salt

1 pound fresh jumbo shrimp

Oil for frying

Lime wedges

1. In a large bowl, combine the olive oil, garlic, cilantro, ginger, hot pepper flakes, lime zest, and salt.

2. Peel and devein the shrimp under cold water, leaving the tails on. Pat dry on paper towels. Add the shrimp to the marinade and toss to coat. Cover the bowl with plastic wrap and refrigerate for up to 2 hours, turning occasionally.

3. Pour 1 inch of oil into a deep fryer. Heat to 375°F. Place 5 to 6 shrimp in the fryer basket without crowding. Lower the basket into the hot oil and fry just until the shrimp turn pink and curl, about 1½ to 2 minutes. Drain on paper towels. Keep warm while frying the remaining shrimp. Serve hot with lime wedges to squeeze over the shrimp.

Fried Catfish with Rémoulade Sauce

Cornmeal-crusted fillet of catfish is a Southern favorite. You can substitute any firm-fleshed white fish of your choice.

MAKES 4 SERVINGS

¾ cup yellow cornmeal
¼ cup all-purpose flour
2 teaspoons salt
1 teaspoon cayenne
⅓ cup milk

4 (6-ounce) catfish fillets
Oil for frying
Rémoulade Sauce (recipe follows) and
    lemon wedges, as accompaniments

1. On a sheet of wax paper, mix the cornmeal, flour, salt, and cayenne. Pour the milk into a pie plate.

2. Lightly score the skinned sides of the fillets 3 or 4 times with a sharp knife. Dip the fillets into the milk, then dredge in the cornmeal mixture to coat. Dip the fillets in the milk a second time and again in the cornmeal to coat thoroughly. Place on a wire rack set over a baking sheet. Let stand at room temperature 30 minutes to set the crumbs.

3. Pour 1½ inches of oil into a deep fryer. Heat to 375°F. Carefully lower 1 fillet into the hot oil. Fry 5 to 6 minutes, until the fish is crisp and golden brown. Lift out the fillet with a wide slotted metal spatula. Drain on paper towels. Keep warm while frying the remaining fillets. Serve with Rémoulade Sauce and lemon wedges on the side.

Rémoulade Sauce

A classic rémoulade contains chopped hard-cooked egg; I have made it optional. This sauce is good with any fish. It can also be served as a dip for crudités.

MAKES 1¼ CUPS

1 cup mayonnaise or creamy salad
  dressing
2 tablespoons drained chopped capers
2 tablespoons chopped cornichons or
  sweet gherkins
2 tablespoons chopped fresh parsley

1 teaspoon Dijon mustard
1 teaspoon anchovy paste or 1 flat
  anchovy, minced, or more to taste
1 hard-cooked egg, finely chopped
  (optional)

In a medium bowl, combine the mayonnaise, capers, cornichons, parsley, mustard, and anchovy paste. Blend in the chopped cooked egg. Cover and refrigerate at least 1 hour for the flavors to mellow.

Mixed Fish Fry

Any fish restaurant worth its salt offers a mixed fried fish platter. This one contains scallops, shrimp, and sole, which are each fried separately. The addition of French Fries (page 125) and creamy coleslaw will round out the meal nicely.

MAKES 6 SERVINGS

1 pound fillet of sole or flounder
1 pound sea scallops
1 pound large shrimp, shelled and
  deveined, leaving the tails on
2 eggs
1 teaspoon salt
½ teaspoon white pepper

½ teaspoon paprika
½ cup all-purpose flour
1½ cups plain dry bread crumbs
Oil for frying
Chili-Horseradish Sauce (recipe follows)
  or Rémoulade Sauce (page 97) and
  lemon wedges

1. Rinse all the seafood under cold water. Pat completely dry on paper towels. Cut the fish fillets crosswise in half.

2. In a pie plate, beat the eggs with 3 tablespoons of water, the salt, pepper, and paprika. Place the flour and the bread crumbs on separate pieces of wax paper.

3. Dredge the seafood in the seasoned flour; shake off any excess. Dip the seafood into the egg mixture, then coat thoroughly in bread crumbs. Set the seafood on a wire rack set over a baking sheet. Let stand at room temperature 30 minutes to set.

4. Pour 1 inch of oil into a deep fryer. Heat to 375°F. Place 2 to 3 fillet pieces in the fryer basket. Gently lower into the hot oil. The oil will bubble up, so be careful. Fry the fish 1 to 2 minutes, until golden brown. Lift the fish out with a large slotted metal spatula. Drain on paper towels. Keep warm while frying the remaining fillets. When frying the scallops and shrimp, place several pieces in the fryer basket without crowding. Cook the scallops and shrimp 1½ to 2 minutes, until golden. Serve hot, with Chili-Horseradish Sauce or Rémoulade Sauce and lemon wedges to squeeze over.

Chili-Horseradish Sauce

This classic seafood cocktail sauce is perfect with any fried fish. It keeps well for up to a week in the refrigerator.

MAKES ⅔ CUP

½ cup bottled chili sauce

1 tablespoon fresh lemon juice

1 to 2 tablespoons drained prepared white horseradish

½ teaspoon hot pepper sauce

½ teaspoon Worcestershire sauce (optional)

In a small bowl, combine all the ingredients. Stir to blend well. Cover and refrigerate at least 30 minutes for the flavors to mellow.

Herb Fried Scallops

These large sea scallops are coated with a light beer batter accented with herbs. The beer batter can also be used to coat clams, shrimp, or fish fillets. I like to serve this with fresh asparagus and rice.

MAKES 6 SERVINGS

¾ cup all-purpose flour
½ teaspoon salt
½ cup flat beer
1 teaspoon vegetable oil
1 egg, separated
2 tablespoons chopped fresh parsley

1½ teaspoons minced fresh tarragon or
   ¾ teaspoon dried
1 teaspoon minced fresh chives
1½ pounds sea scallops
Oil for frying
Lemon or lime wedges

1. In a medium bowl, combine the flour and salt. Stir in the beer and oil. Cover and let stand at room temperature 3 to 4 hours.

2. In a small bowl, beat the egg white until stiff peaks form. In another small bowl, beat the egg yolk, parsley, tarragon, and chives. Beat the egg yolk mixture into the beer batter. Fold in the beaten egg white.

3. Rinse the scallops in a colander with cold water. Pat dry with paper towels.

4. Pour 1 inch of oil into a deep fryer. Heat to 375°F. Place a few scallops in the beer batter and turn to coat. Lift the scallops out, 1 at a time, with a fork and tap the fork against the side of the bowl to remove excess batter. Place 4 or 5 scallops in the hot oil. Fry the scallops, turning once, 3½ to 4 minutes, or until golden. Drain on paper towels. Keep warm while frying the remaining scallops. Serve hot with lemon or lime wedges to squeeze over the scallops.

Goujonette of Flounder

The word goujonette *is taken from the French for gudgeon, a small freshwater fish, which is usually fried whole. It can also refer to any fish that is cut into thin strips. Here strips of flounder are coated with an herb-flavored crumb mixture and, when fried, curl up into interesting shapes.*

MAKES 3 OR 4 SERVINGS

4 fillets of flounder or sole (about 5 ounces each)
Salt and pepper
½ cup unseasoned dry bread crumbs
2 tablespoons minced fresh parsley
¼ teaspoon dried rosemary

¼ teaspoon dried thyme leaves
¼ cup all-purpose flour
2 eggs
Oil for frying
Lemon wedges

1. Rinse the fillets with cold water. Pat dry with paper towels. Sprinkle the fillets with salt and pepper. Cut each fillet lengthwise into 4 strips.

2. On wax paper, combine the bread crumbs, parsley, rosemary, and thyme. On another piece of wax paper, place the flour. In a pie plate, beat the eggs with 2 tablespoons of water until well combined.

3. Dredge the fish strips in the flour. Dip the fish into the beaten egg, then coat thoroughly in the herbed bread crumbs. Place on a wire rack set over a baking sheet. Let stand at room temperature 30 minutes to set the crumbs.

4. Pour 1 inch of oil into a deep fryer. Heat to 375°F. Fry the fish strips, a few pieces at a time, in the hot oil about 1 minute. Drain on paper towels. Keep warm while frying the remaining fish. Serve hot with lemon wedges to squeeze over.

Salt Codfish Cakes

The traditional components of codfish cakes are equal amounts of cod and mashed potatoes. The interest in Cuban and Hispanic cuisines has spurred the comeback of salt cod, which is called bacalao. *Since salt cod is preserved in salt, you need to soak it overnight and change the water at least once. In Maryland, breaded and deep-fried cod cakes are called "coddees."*

MAKES 8 CAKES

1 (1-pound) package salt cod
   (bacalao)
¾ pound all-purpose potatoes, peeled
   and cut into 1-inch cubes
4 tablespoons butter
½ cup minced onion
½ cup minced celery

¼ teaspoon salt
¼ teaspoon pepper
1 egg, separated
½ cup all-purpose flour
½ cup cracker crumbs or unseasoned
   dry bread crumbs
Oil for frying

1. Place the codfish in a large bowl with enough cold water to cover. Cover the bowl with plastic wrap or foil and refrigerate 8 hours or overnight, changing the water at least once.

2. Drain the cod and place in a single layer in a large skillet. Add fresh cold water to cover. Bring the water to a boil over high heat. Reduce the heat to low and simmer 15 minutes, or until the cod flakes easily when pierced with a fork. Drain and let cool.

3. Meanwhile, in a medium saucepan, cook the potatoes in unsalted water to cover 10 to 15 minutes, or until fork-tender; drain. Return the potatoes to the saucepan and place over heat. Heat the potatoes 1 minute while mashing with a fork until smooth. Place the potatoes in a large bowl.

4. Melt the butter in a medium saucepan. Add the onion and celery; cook over medium heat, stirring occasionally, until softened, about 5 minutes. Add the vegetables to the potatoes in the bowl.

5. Remove the skin and bones from the cod. Flake the cod and add to the potatoes with the salt, pepper, and egg yolk. Beat together until well combined. Season with additional salt and pepper to taste. With slightly moistened hands, shape the cod mixture into 8 cakes about 3 inches in diameter. If the mixture is too soft, refrigerate 15 minutes.

6. Place the flour and cracker or bread crumbs on separate pieces of wax paper. In a pie plate, beat the egg white with 1 tablespoon water until foamy.

7. Dredge the cod cakes in the flour, then dip in the beaten egg white. Coat the cod cakes completely with the crumbs. Reshape the cakes and place on a wire rack set over a baking sheet. Cover and refrigerate 1 hour to firm up.

8. Pour 1 inch of oil into a deep fryer. Heat to 375°F. Place 2 or 3 codfish cakes in the fryer basket and lower into the hot oil. Fry the cod cakes 2 minutes, until golden and done. Drain on paper towels. Serve hot.

Fish and Chips

I first tasted this classic fried fish and french fry combination on my first trip to England, where it was served in a brown paper cone, sprinkled with malt vinegar. You can use a variety of fish, such as halibut, striped bass, perch, catfish, or orange roughy, instead of the cod. While it is possible to use frozen french fries, this dish of fish and chips warrants making freshly made french fried potatoes. When frying fish and potatoes, the oil should always be at 375°F.

MAKES 4 SERVINGS

1 cup all-purpose flour
1 teaspoon salt
1 teaspoon paprika
⅛ teaspoon pepper
6 ounces flat beer
1½ pounds cod or halibut fillets, cut
   ¾ to 1 inch thick

¼ cup fresh lemon juice
2 tablespoons grated onion
Oil for frying
4 medium baking potatoes (6 ounces
   each), about 4 inches long
Malt vinegar or lemon wedges

1. In a medium bowl, combine the flour, salt, paprika, and pepper. Remove ½ cup of the seasoned flour and place on a sheet of wax paper.

2. Whisk the beer into the seasoned flour in the bowl and let stand at room temperature 1 hour. The batter will be thin.

3. Cut the fish into ¾-inch-wide pieces. In a shallow dish large enough to hold the fish in a single layer, combine the lemon juice with the onion. Place the fish sticks in the lemon mixture and turn to coat. Let stand at room temperature 30 minutes.

4. Pour 1½ inches of oil into a deep fryer. Heat to 375°F.

5. While the oil is heating, peel the potatoes and cut into ¼-inch sticks. Pat the potatoes with paper towels until thoroughly dry. Place one-third of the potatoes in the fryer basket and gradually lower into the hot oil. The oil will bubble up slightly, so be careful. Fry the potatoes until just tender but not brown, about 2 minutes. Drain on paper towels. The potatoes should yield slightly when pressed with your finger. Repeat with the remaining potatoes.

6. Dredge the fish in the reserved seasoned flour. Coat 1 piece of fish at a time with the beer batter. Lift the fish out of the batter with tongs or a slotted metal spoon; let the excess batter drip back into the bowl. If the batter is sliding off the fish, whisk in an additional tablespoon of flour. Place the fish in the hot oil and fry, 4 pieces at a time, until lightly golden, about 2 minutes. Shake the fryer basket at the beginning of the frying time to prevent the fish from sticking to the basket. Drain on paper towels. Keep warm while frying the remaining fish.

7. Return half of the potatoes to the hot oil and fry until golden brown, about 2 minutes. Drain on paper towels. Keep warm while frying the remaining potatoes. Serve the fish and chips drizzled with malt vinegar or lemon wedges to squeeze over.

Fish Fingers with Garlic Sauce

For uniform fish fingers, buy the thickest cut of scrod (cod) you can find. Prepare the sauce first before frying the fish.

MAKES 6 SERVINGS

2½ pounds thick scrod, cod, haddock, halibut, or orange roughy fillets
1 cup all-purpose flour
½ teaspoon salt
¼ teaspoon baking powder

⅛ teaspoon white pepper
¾ to 1 cup ice water
Oil for frying
Garlic Sauce (recipe follows)

1. Cut the fish into 6 serving-size pieces. Rinse the fish pieces under cold water and pat dry with paper towels.

2. In a medium bowl, combine the flour, salt, baking powder, and pepper. Whisk in the water to make a slightly thick, but lumpy batter. Let the batter stand at room temperature for 15 minutes.

3. Pour 1½ inches of oil into a deep fryer. Heat to 375°F.

4. Dip the fish, 1 piece at a time, into the batter to coat. Lift the fish out with a slotted metal spoon, letting the excess batter drip back into the bowl. Slide the fish into the hot oil and fry, 2 pieces at a time, until lightly golden, 3 to 5 minutes. Drain on paper towels. Keep warm while frying the remaining fish. Serve with Garlic Sauce on the side.

Garlic Sauce

This is an easy version of a Greek sauce called skordalia. *It is good on any bland fish, and can also be served as a dip for raw vegetables or spooned over steamed vegetables.*

MAKES 1½ CUPS

8 slices of firm-textured white bread,
    crusts removed
½ cup cold water
4 garlic cloves
½ teaspoon salt

⅓ cup fresh lemon juice
½ cup olive oil or ¼ cup *each*
    regular olive oil and extra-virgin
    olive oil

1. In a large bowl, sprinkle each bread slice with 1 tablespoon of the water. Let stand briefly, then squeeze the excess water from the bread.

2. In a food processor, whirl the garlic with the salt until finely chopped. Add the moistened bread and the lemon juice. Process until smooth. Slowly drizzle in the oil through the feeder tube until the sauce has thickened and is smooth. Pour the sauce into a serving bowl. Cover and refrigerate until ready to use.

Fried Soft-Shell Crabs With
Lemon-Basil Butter

Soft-shell crabs are not a species, but rather blue crabs that are molting, or shedding, their hard outer shell. They are usually available from mid-May through August. Have the fishmonger clean them or do it yourself (see below). Once cleaned, they should be cooked within 4 hours.

MAKES 4 SERVINGS

---

1 cup all-purpose flour

1 teaspoon salt

¼ teaspoon cayenne

2 eggs

½ cup milk

1 cup cracker crumbs

8 soft-shell crabs (about 4 ounces
    each), cleaned and patted dry

Oil for frying

8 large fresh basil leaves with ¼-inch
    stems, rinsed and patted dry
    (optional garnish)

Lemon-Basil Butter (recipe follows)

Lemon slices

1. On wax paper, combine the flour, salt, and cayenne. In a pie plate, beat the eggs with the milk. Place the cracker crumbs on another sheet of wax paper.

2. Dredge the crabs thoroughly in the flour; shake off the excess. Dip the crabs in the beaten eggs and coat completely with the cracker crumbs. Set on a wire rack.

3. Pour 1½ inches of oil into a deep fryer. Heat to 375°F. If using the basil, place 4 of the leaves in the fryer basket and gently lower into the hot oil. Be careful as the oil will splatter. Fry the leaves about 45 seconds, or just until they begin to turn a deep green and look crisp. Lift the basil leaves out with a slotted metal spoon and drain on paper towels. They are fragile, so handle gently.

---

4. Place the crabs, 2 at a time, in the hot oil. Fry 3 to 4 minutes, until golden and crisp. Drain on paper towels. Keep warm while frying the remaining crabs. To serve, place the crabs on a platter or place 2 on each of 4 plates. Drizzle with Lemon-Basil Butter. Garnish with the fried basil leaves and lemon slices.

TO CLEAN CRABS: With scissors, remove the eyes and the mouth behind the eyes, then the gills found under both sides of the shell. Turn the crab over and cut off the "apron"— the flap that folds under the body. Rinse and pat *very* dry.

Lemon-Basil Butter

8 tablespoons (1 stick) butter
¼ cup fresh lemon juice

¼ cup chopped fresh basil

In a small skillet over low heat, melt the butter. Stir in the lemon juice and basil. Serve at once.

Fried Oysters

Plump and tender fresh oysters in a crispy coating are irresistible. They taste good with just a drizzle of lemon juice or hot sauce, but you can also dip them in the Chili-Horseradish Sauce (page 99), if you like.

MAKES 4 MAIN-COURSE OR 8 APPETIZER SERVINGS

1 egg
1 tablespoon milk or water
2 teaspoons Chesapeake Bay-style
  seafood seasoning
½ cup all-purpose flour

½ cup cracker crumbs
24 shucked oysters, drained
Oil for frying
Lemon wedges and hot pepper sauce

1. In a pie plate, beat the egg with the milk or water and 1 teaspoon of the seafood seasoning. On wax paper, combine the flour with the remaining 1 teaspoon seafood seasoning. Place the cracker crumbs on another sheet of wax paper.

2. Dredge the oysters, 1 at a time, in the flour. Dip in the beaten egg and then roll in the crumbs to coat completely; use a fork to help roll the oysters in the crumbs. Place on a wire rack.

3. Pour 1½ inches of oil into a deep fryer. Heat to 375°F. Fry the oysters 4 or 5 at a time, until golden and crisp, 1 to 1½ minutes. Drain on paper towels. Serve hot with lemon wedges and hot sauce.

Clam Fritters

This classic clam fritter recipe uses canned minced clams for a quick and easy dish. One cup fresh-shucked, finely chopped clams can be substituted.

MAKES 3 (6-FRITTER) SERVINGS

Oil for frying
2 (8-ounce) cans minced clams
¾ cup all-purpose flour
1 teaspoon baking powder
¼ teaspoon salt
¼ teaspoon cayenne

¼ cup milk
1 egg
2 tablespoons minced onion
Chili-Horseradish Sauce (page 99)
Lemon wedges

1. Pour 1½ inches of oil into a deep fryer. Heat to 375°F.

2. Drain the clams, reserving ¼ cup of the clam liquid. Freeze the remaining clam liquid for another use.

3. In a large bowl, combine the flour, baking powder, salt, and cayenne. In a small bowl, beat together the milk, egg, and the reserved ¼ cup clam juice. Stir into the flour mixture just until combined. Stir in the drained clams and the onion.

4. Drop the batter by level tablespoons into the hot oil. Fry the fritters 4 or 5 at a time for 3 to 4 minutes, until golden and cooked through in the center. Drain on paper towels. Keep warm while frying the remaining fritters. Serve with Chili-Horseradish Sauce and lemon wedges to squeeze over the fritters.

Fried Clams

Have the fishmonger shuck the clams unless you are an expert at doing this.

MAKES 4 SERVINGS

1 quart shucked hard-shelled clams
1 egg
2 teaspoons Chesapeake Bay-style
  seafood seasoning
½ cup all-purpose flour
¾ to 1 cup cracker crumbs or dry
  bread crumbs

Oil for frying
Chili-Horseradish Sauce (page 99) or
  Rémoulade Sauce (page 97)
Lemon wedges

1. Drain the clams, reserving 2 tablespoons of the clam liquid. Strain the remaining liquid and freeze for another use.

2. In a pie plate, beat together the egg, seafood seasoning, and the reserved 2 tablespoons clam juice with a fork until well mixed. On separate sheets of wax paper, place the flour and the cracker crumbs.

3. Dredge the clams, 1 at a time, in the flour. Dip the clams in the beaten seasoned eggs, then roll in the crumbs, using a fork. Place on a wire rack.

4. Pour 1½ inches of oil into a deep fryer. Heat to 375°F. Fry the clams, 4 or 5 at a time, until golden and crisp, 1½ to 2 minutes. Drain on paper towels. Keep warm while frying the remaining clams. Serve with Chili-Horseradish Sauce or Rémoulade Sauce and lemon wedges to squeeze over.

Tempura

The secret of a good Japanese tempura is in the batter, which must be undermixed and made at the last moment. The tiny lumps of unmixed flour puff up around the vegetables and seafood in the hot oil. A variety of vegetables, such as fingers of eggplant, carrot sticks, string beans, and small pieces of squash, can be substituted for or added to those listed below. Prepare the dipping sauce and have all the vegetables and seafood set out on a tray before mixing the batter. Fry each vegetable and the fish separately.

MAKES 4 GENEROUS SERVINGS

1½ cups cake flour

1½ teaspoons baking powder

½ teaspoon salt

1 egg white

1¼ cups ice water

Oil for frying

1 medium sweet potato, pared and cut into ¼-inch slices

1 medium red or green bell pepper, seeded and cut into ½-inch strips

1 small red onion, cut into ¼-inch slices and slices separated

8 medium shiitake mushrooms, stems removed

1 pound large shrimp, shelled and deveined, or 1 pound sea scallops or 1 pound fish fillets, cut into 3 × 2-inch pieces, patted dry

Tempura Dipping Sauce (recipe follows)

1. On wax paper, combine the flour, baking powder, and salt. In a medium bowl, blend the egg white with the water. Sift the flour mixture into the water, stirring just until moistened and leaving the batter slightly lumpy.

2. Pour 1½ inches of oil into a deep fryer. Heat to 375°F.

3. Dip the vegetables and the seafood, a few pieces at a time, into the batter, letting the excess batter drip back into the bowl. Fry the vegetables until lightly golden, 3 to

4 minutes; seafood, 2 to 3 minutes. Drain on paper towels. Keep warm while frying the remaining batches of vegetables and fish. Remove bits of loose batter from the frying oil. Serve at once, with small bowls of Tempura Dipping Sauce for each person.

Tempura Dipping Sauce

MAKES 1⅓ CUPS

1 cup chicken broth
⅓ cup Japanese soy sauce or reduced-
    sodium soy sauce
⅓ cup mirin or dry sherry

1½ teaspoons sugar
1 teaspoon grated fresh ginger
2 tablespoons sliced scallions

In a small saucepan, combine the chicken broth, soy sauce, mirin, sugar, and ginger. Bring to a boil over low heat. Simmer, uncovered, 5 minutes. Remove from the heat and let cool. Add the scallions.

Creole Crab and Rice Cakes

MAKES 4 (2-CRAB CAKE) SERVINGS

3 eggs

2 tablespoons minced fresh parsley

2 tablespoons minced red bell pepper

2 tablespoons minced scallions

2 tablespoons mayonnaise

1 tablespoon white wine Worcestershire sauce

1 tablespoon Creole mustard or Dijon-style mustard with horseradish

½ teaspoon cayenne

1 cup cooked long-grain white rice, at room temperature

1 cup cracker crumbs

2 (6-ounce) cans fancy lump crabmeat, drained well, or 12 ounces fresh crab-meat, picked over, or crabmeat substi-tute, squeezed dry and coarsely chopped

¼ cup all-purpose flour

Oil for frying

Lemon or lime wedges

1. In a medium bowl, beat 2 of the eggs. Beat in the parsley, red bell pepper, scallions, mayonnaise, Worcestershire sauce, mustard, and cayenne. Stir in the rice and ¼ cup of the cracker crumbs. Gently fold in the crabmeat. Shape into eight ½-inch patties, about ⅓ cup each.

2. In a pie plate, beat the remaining egg with 1 tablespoon water until foamy. On separate sheets of wax paper, place the flour and the remaining ¾ cup cracker crumbs.

3. Coat each crab cake thoroughly with the flour. Dip the crab cakes into the egg and coat each thoroughly with the cracker crumbs. Place on a wax paper-lined wire rack. Refrigerate until firm, about 1 hour. Remove the crab cakes from the refrigerator while heating the oil.

4. Pour 1½ inches of oil into a deep fryer. Heat to 375°F. Slide the crab cakes into the hot oil, using a wide slotted metal spatula. Fry 2 or 3 crab cakes at a time in the hot oil 3 minutes, or until golden, turning once. Remove the crab cakes from the oil with the spatula. Drain on paper towels. Keep warm while frying the remaining crab cakes. Serve hot with lemon or lime wedges to squeeze over.

Vegetables, Grains, and Potatoes

The array of vegetables that can be cooked in a deep fryer varies only with the bounty of the season. Since vegetables cooked in the machine are either encased in a batter or crumb coated, their nutrients are not lost. Vegetables come out of the hot oil crunchy on the outside and crisp-tender on the inside. You can fry up such popular favorites as sweet potatoes, onion rings, and zucchini strips. But you can also feature some more exotic additions to the vegetable basket, such as plantains, artichokes, and green tomatoes. To ensure that the vegetables fry up to a golden crispness in the time allotted in each recipe, they must be cut the same size, whether into sticks, rounds, florets, or strips. If a recipe calls for more than one type of vegetable, fry each vegetable separately.

The two-step method of frying potatoes in the deep fryer will give you crisp and golden-brown fries or matchsticks. The method involves frying the potatoes at a low temperature to release the water in them and to soften them, then frying them at 375°F. to crisp and brown them. You won't make potatoes any other way once you try this method.

Hints and Tips

- Vegetables must be patted dry to allow the batter or crumbs to adhere.
- Don't crowd the fryer basket during frying as the result will be steamed vegetables.
- Bring the oil temperature back to the recommended temperature between batches.

Vegetable Fritto Misto

This Italian extravaganza always makes a big hit. Serve it as a main dish or as an appetizer and substitute any vegetables you like—canned or frozen artichoke hearts, blanched baby carrots, fennel, eggplant cubes, or mushrooms—for some of those listed in the recipe below.

MAKES 6 SERVINGS

1⅓ cups sifted all-purpose flour

2 tablespoons grated Parmesan or Romano cheese

½ teaspoon salt

1¼ cups flat beer, at room temperature

2 eggs, separated

1 tablespoon olive oil

3 tablespoons chopped fresh oregano or 2 teaspoons dried

1 garlic clove, crushed through a press

Oil for frying

3 cups broccoli florets (8 ounces)

3 cups cauliflower florets (8 ounces)

1 large red bell pepper, cut into ¾-inch strips

1 small zucchini, cut crosswise on an angle into ½-inch slices

12 pitted jumbo black olives, patted dry (½ cup)

1. In a large bowl, stir together the flour, cheese, and salt. In a medium bowl, whisk together the beer, egg yolks, oil, oregano, and garlic. Whisk into the flour mixture until smooth.

2. In a medium bowl, beat the egg whites until stiff peaks form. Fold the beaten whites into the beer batter.

3. Pour 1½ inches of oil into a deep fryer. Heat to 375°F. Working in batches without crowding, dip the vegetables into the batter with tongs; let the excess drip back into the bowl. Lower into the hot oil and fry, turning once, until golden, 3 to 4 minutes. Drain on paper towels. Keep warm in a 200°F. oven. Stir the batter several times during frying to keep it evenly mixed. Add the olives to the remaining batter in the bowl; toss to coat and fry all at once in the hot oil. Serve immediately.

Falafel with Lemon Tahini Sauce

In city streets, umbrella-topped pushcarts entice lunchtime crowds with this easy-to-eat, lunch-on-the-run pita sandwich. It is important to keep the frying temperature at 375°F. to prevent the falafel from coming apart in the oil.

MAKES 8 SERVINGS

1 (19-ounce) can chickpeas
1 cup finely chopped onion
2 garlic cloves, crushed through a press
2 teaspoons ground coriander
2 teaspoons ground cumin
1 teaspoon salt
1 teaspoon crushed hot pepper flakes
½ teaspoon turmeric
1 cup unseasoned dry bread crumbs

2 tablespoons minced fresh parsley
Oil for frying
8 pita breads
2 cups shredded romaine lettuce
1 cup diced tomato
Red onion slices, radish sprouts, and diced cucumber (optional)
Lemon Tahini Sauce (recipe follows) or plain yogurt

1. Drain the chickpeas, reserving ¼ cup of the liquid. Place the chickpeas, reserved liquid, onion, garlic, coriander, cumin, salt, hot pepper, and turmeric in a food processor. Puree until smooth. You may have to turn off the food processor and scrape down the sides of the container.

2. Turn the chickpea puree into a large bowl. Stir in the bread crumbs and parsley. Form about 2 level tablespoons of the mixture at a time into 1½-inch balls. Flatten slightly to 2-inch patties.

3. Pour 1 inch of oil into a deep fryer. Heat to 375°F. Fry the patties in batches without crowding until deep golden brown, about 2 minutes. Drain on paper towels.

4. To serve: Warm the pita breads in the oven or microwave. Cut a thin slice off the top and open up the pocket. Drop in 3 or 4 falafel. Tuck in some lettuce and tomato and add any accompaniments desired. Top with Lemon Tahini Sauce and serve.

Lemon Tahini Sauce

This is the classic sauce for falafel, which can double as a dip for fresh raw vegetables or pita triangles, or as a salad dressing with greens.

MAKES 1⅓ CUPS

½ cup plain yogurt
½ cup tahini (Middle Eastern sesame paste)

¼ cup fresh lemon juice
4 garlic cloves, crushed through a press

Place the yogurt, tahini, lemon juice, garlic, and ¼ cup water in a food processor. Puree until smooth. Turn into a bowl. Cover and refrigerate at least 1 hour for the flavors to mellow.

Tostones

Tostones are fried green plantains, which can be served as a side dish or as a starch in place of potatoes or rice. Or pass them as a hot appetizer.

MAKES 4 TO 6 SERVINGS

Oil for frying
2 large green plantains (about 12
  ounces each)

Salt

1. Pour 1 inch of oil into a deep fryer. Heat to 375°F.

2. To remove the skin from the plantains, cut the tips off the ends. Cut a slit along the length of the plantain and peel off the skin. Cut the plantains crosswise on an angle into oval slices 1 inch thick.

3. Place one-third of the plantain slices in the fryer basket in a single layer. Carefully lower into the hot oil. Fry the slices just until they begin to get creamy looking and start to brown. Drain on paper towels. Let cool while you fry the remaining slices.

4. On a work surface, flatten each plantain slice with the bottom of a large glass to a ½-inch thickness or place the slices between 2 sheets of wax paper and press down with the heel of your hand. The edges of the plantain will become slightly irregular.

5. Return the plantains to the hot oil, in batches without crowding, and fry until golden, about 3 to 4 minutes. Drain on paper towels and while they're still hot, season with salt to taste. Serve at once.

French-Fried Okra

Oil for frying
1 pound fresh okra (about 4 inches long)
2 eggs

½ cup self-rising flour
½ teaspoon salt
¼ teaspoon cayenne

1. Pour 1 inch of oil into a deep fryer. Heat to 375°F.

2. Meanwhile, rinse the okra and pat dry with paper towels. Trim off the stems and tips.

3. In a pie plate, beat the eggs until thoroughly combined. In a large plastic food storage bag, combine the flour, salt, and cayenne. Dip the okra, a few at a time, in the eggs, then shake well in the seasoned flour to coat.

4. Fry the okra in batches without crowding 3 to 4 minutes, until golden brown, turning once or twice. Drain on paper towels. Serve warm.

French-Fried Sweet Potato Sticks

Whether you sprinkle these tasty fried sweet potato sticks with salt or cinnamon sugar, they make a fine accompaniment to pork chops, ham, or turkey.

MAKES 4 TO 6 SERVINGS

Oil for frying

4 medium-size sweet potatoes (2 pounds total), each 6 to 7 inches long

Coarse (kosher) salt or Cinnamon Sugar (page 172)

1. Pour 1½ inches of oil into a deep fryer. Heat to 350°F.

2. Peel the sweet potatoes and trim off the ends. With a sharp knife, cut lengthwise into long sticks 6 × ½ × ½-inch. Pat dry on paper towels.

3. Fry a handful of sweet potatoes at a time, 3 minutes per batch, or until crisp and golden. Drain on paper towels. Sprinkle with salt or Cinnamon Sugar. Serve at once while still warm.

French Fries

Arguably, this is the most popular way potatoes are eaten in America. In France, french fries are called pommes frites, *in England "chips." The term "french fry" refers to "frenching," the method of cutting the potatoes into narrow strips. The two-step method of frying potatoes that I give below ensures a crisp fry. You can prepare the potatoes early in the day and then finish up the frying just before you're ready to eat.*

MAKES 4 SERVINGS

4 medium baking potatoes, such as Russets or Idahos (1½ pounds total)

Salt
Oil for frying

1. Scrub the potatoes well under cold water; do not peel. Cut into large fries using the french-fry blade of a vegetable slicer or mandoline, or cut with a sharp knife into ¼- to ½-inch strips about 4 inches long.

2. Place the potato strips in a large bowl filled with 4 cups water and 1 teaspoon salt. Add 4 to 6 ice cubes. Let stand at room temperature or place in the refrigerator for 1 hour.

3. Pour 1½ inches of oil into a deep fryer. Heat to 325° to 330°F.

4. Drain the potatoes and pat very dry with paper towels to prevent the hot oil from spattering when they are added. Place a handful of potatoes in the fryer basket. Gently lower into the hot oil. Be careful as the oil will bubble up. Fry 4 to 5 minutes, until the potatoes are pale gold; do not brown. Drain on paper towels. Repeat with the remaining potatoes. Set aside at room temperature.

5. When almost ready to serve, heat the oil to 375°F. Fry the potatoes in 2 or 3 batches for 3 to 4 minutes per batch, until golden brown. Drain on paper towels. Sprinkle with salt while still warm. Serve at once.

Fried Green Tomatoes with Aioli and Pancetta

The abundance of green tomatoes during the summer warrants making this dish. Aioli, a garlic mayonnaise, and pancetta, an unsmoked Italian bacon, top these cornmeal-crusted rings.

MAKES 4 SERVINGS

2 ounces pancetta or slab bacon, diced
¼ cup all-purpose flour
¼ teaspoon salt
¼ teaspoon pepper
½ to ¾ cup yellow cornmeal, preferably stone ground
2 tablespoons finely chopped fresh oregano or 2 teaspoons dried

1 egg
4 medium green tomatoes (6 ounces each), all the same size
Oil for frying
Aioli (recipe follows)

1. In a medium skillet, cook the pancetta over low heat until crisp, 10 to 12 minutes. Drain on paper towels.

2. On a sheet of wax paper, combine the flour, salt, and pepper. Mix the cornmeal and oregano on another sheet. In a shallow bowl, beat the egg until well blended.

3. Rinse and dry the tomatoes. Cut a thin slice off the top and bottom of each tomato. Cut each tomato into 3 thick slices.

4. Dredge the tomato slices in the seasoned flour. Dip in the egg and then coat thoroughly with cornmeal. Place on a wire rack set over a baking sheet.

5. Pour 1 inch of oil into a deep fryer. Heat to 375°F. Fry 3 or 4 tomato slices at a time, 3 minutes on each side, until lightly golden. Drain on paper towels. Serve warm, topped with a dollop of Aioli and a sprinkling of pancetta.

Aioli

This is a short-cut version of aioli, the silky Provençal garlic mayonnaise. While I suggest it for fried green tomatoes, it is also good dolloped on fish, potatoes, and almost any vegetable.

MAKES ½ CUP

½ cup mayonnaise
2 garlic cloves, crushed through a
   press

1 tablespoon fresh lemon juice

In a small bowl, combine all the ingredients. Mix to blend well. Cover and refrigerate until ready to use.

Matchstick Potatoes

These are golden brown and crisp, just like those you get in the fanciest restaurants. Serve with grilled steak and garden-fresh ripe tomatoes.

MAKES 4 TO 6 SERVINGS

4 medium baking potatoes, such as   Salt
    Russets or Idahos (1½ pounds total)   Oil for frying

1. Peel the potatoes and cut them into matchsticks, using the matchstick blade of a vegetable cutter or mandoline, or cut with a sharp knife into ⅛-inch strips about 3 inches long.

2. Place the potatoes in a large bowl filled with 4 cups of cold water and 1 teaspoon salt. Add 4 to 6 ice cubes. Let stand at room temperature or place in the refrigerator for 1 hour.

3. Pour 1½ inches of oil into a deep fryer. Heat to 325° to 330°F.

4. Drain the potatoes and pat very dry with paper towels to prevent the hot oil from spattering when they are added. Place one-third of the potatoes in the fryer basket. Gently lower into the hot fat. Be careful as the oil will bubble up. Fry 4 to 5 minutes, or until the potatoes are pale gold; do not brown. Drain on paper towels. Repeat with the remaining 2 batches. Set aside at room temperature.

5. When almost ready to serve, heat the oil to 375°F. Fry half of the potatoes 1 minute, or until crisp and golden brown. Drain on paper towels. Sprinkle with salt while still warm. Repeat with the remaining potatoes. Serve at once.

Potato Croquettes with
Goat Cheese and Scallions

You can prepare these savory potato logs early in the day and fry them just before you are ready to serve them. These can also be served as a hot appetizer.

MAKES 4 OR 5 SERVINGS (20 CROQUETTES)

1½ pounds baking potatoes, peeled
  and cut into ¼-inch cubes
1 teaspoon salt
3 ounces mild white goat cheese, such
  as Montrachet
⅓ cup finely chopped scallions

¼ teaspoon cracked black pepper
1 egg
2 to 3 tablespoons all-purpose flour
⅓ cup unseasoned dry bread crumbs
Oil for frying

1. In a medium saucepan, boil the potatoes with ½ teaspoon of the salt and enough cold water to cover 10 minutes, or until the potatoes are tender. Drain and return the potatoes to the saucepan. Cook over low heat to dry, mashing the potatoes with a fork until there are no lumps. Remove from the heat and cool.

2. Add the goat cheese, scallions, pepper, and remaining ½ teaspoon salt to the potatoes. Beat until well blended. Using 2 level tablespoons of the potato mixture at a time, shape into 2-inch logs.

3. In a pie plate, beat the egg with 1 tablespoon of water until well blended. Place the flour and bread crumbs on separate sheets of wax paper.

4. Gently roll the potato logs in flour; shake off any excess. Dip in the beaten egg, then roll in the bread crumbs to coat completely. Place on a wire rack set over a baking sheet. When all the potato logs are coated, taper the ends to shape into 2½-inch ovals.

5. Pour 1 inch of oil into a deep fryer. Heat to 375°F. Place 5 croquettes in the fryer basket and gently lower into the hot oil. Fry 2 minutes, or until golden. Lift out with a slotted spoon. Drain on paper towels. Keep warm while frying the remaining croquettes.

Crispy Red Onion Shreds

These savory onions make a marvelous topping for meats. They can be sprinkled over mashed potatoes or tucked into a hot sandwich. The onions must be stirred during frying, so keep the fryer cover open. Ordinary yellow onions or shallots can also be prepared the same way.

MAKES 2 CUPS

Oil for frying   ¼ cup all-purpose flour
2 medium red onions

1. Pour 1 inch of oil into a deep fryer. Heat to 350°F.
2. Thinly slice the onions by cutting them in half from stem to root and then lengthwise into thin shreds. Pat dry on paper towels. Place in a bowl. Add the flour and toss to coat.
3. Lift the onions from the flour, letting the excess sift through your fingers. Fry the onions, a handful at a time, until crisp and golden brown, about 5 minutes, stirring occasionally. Drain on paper towels. Serve hot.

Fried Onion Rings

1½ cups all-purpose flour
½ teaspoon salt
⅛ teaspoon pepper
1½ cups flat beer, at room
   temperature

2 large sweet onions (¾ pound each),
   such as Vidalia, Spanish, Texas
   Sweets, or Bermuda
Solid vegetable shortening or oil for
   frying

1. In a large bowl, mix the flour, salt, and pepper. Whisk in the beer until the batter is smooth. Let stand at room temperature 3 hours or longer.

2. Peel the onions and cut into ¼-inch-thick slices. Separate into rings.

3. Place the shortening in small pieces in a deep fryer and melt, following the manufacturer's directions, or pour in 1½ inches of oil. Heat to 375°F.

4. Whisk the batter before using. With metal tongs, dip a few onion rings at a time into the batter. Lift out, letting the excess batter drip back into the bowl. Then carefully place the onions in the hot oil. Fry, turning once or twice, until golden, 2 to 3 minutes. Drain or brown paper-lined baking sheets or on paper towels. Keep warm in a 200°F. oven while frying the remaining onion rings. Stir the batter occasionally. Serve hot.

Fried Whole Artichokes

Roman-style fried artichokes, one of the oldest recipes from the Jewish ghetto in Rome, hearken back to the days of the Empire. These go great with lamb or steak, or they can be served as part of a hot antipasto. They do take time to make, but the effort is worth it.

MAKES 4 SERVINGS

4 medium-sized artichokes (6 to
   8 ounces each)
1 tablespoon fresh lemon juice
Oil for frying

½ teaspoon salt
Pepper
Coarse (kosher) salt

1. Trim the artichoke stems, leaving 1 inch. Bend back the tough outer petals at the base of the artichokes until they snap. Using scissors, cut off the top third of each outer leaf, going all around the artichoke. With a sharp knife, cut off the top of the inner cone of leaves. Remove the tiny white center cone of leaves and, using a grapefruit knife or small curved knife, scrape away and discard the fuzzy center "choke." As you finish each artichoke, place it in a bowl of water to cover along with the lemon juice to prevent darkening.

2. Pour 2 to 2½ inches of oil into a deep fryer. Heat to 300°F.

3. Remove the artichokes from the acidulated water and place upside down on paper towels to drain. Wipe the artichokes dry. Gently press down with palm of your hand to slightly open up the leaves. Turn right side up and sprinkle each lightly with some of the salt and a few grindings of pepper.

4. Place 2 artichokes in the fryer basket and carefully lower into the hot oil. Watch out, because the water that clings to the artichokes will cause the oil to sputter and bubble up. Although you don't want too much water to hit the oil, a little is desirable, as the reaction of the cold water with the hot oil helps to open the leaves slightly. Fry the artichokes 8 to 10 minutes, turning several times between 2 wooden spoons, until the bottoms can be pierced easily with a small knife. Lift the basket from the oil and place the artichokes, stem up, on paper towels to drain. Press down slightly on each artichoke with a wooden spoon to spread the leaves without breaking the artichoke. Repeat with the remaining 2 artichokes.

5. Increase the oil temperature to 375°F. Return the artichokes, 2 at a time, to the oil and fry until golden and crisp, 3 to 5 minutes. Transfer upside down to paper towels to drain. Turn right side up and season with coarse salt to taste. Serve warm.

Fried Zucchini Strips

Zucchini is a versatile vegetable that adapts itself to a variety of cooking methods. Here it is cut into sticks, flavored with Parmesan cheese and basil, and fried into crispy, succulent strips. Try this technique with peeled eggplant strips also.

MAKES 4 SERVINGS

2 medium zucchini
¼ cup all-purpose flour
½ teaspoon dried basil
1 teaspoon salt
½ teaspoon pepper

¾ cup unseasoned dry bread crumbs
¼ cup grated fresh Parmesan cheese
2 eggs
Oil for frying

1. Rinse the zucchini under cold water and pat dry with paper towels. Trim off the ends and cut into ½-inch sticks about 4 inches long.

2. In a shallow bowl, combine the flour, basil, salt, and pepper. On a sheet of wax paper, mix the bread crumbs with the Parmesan cheese. In a pie plate, beat the eggs with 1 teaspoon water until blended.

3. Toss part of the zucchini in the flour mixture; shake off any excess. Dip the zucchini in the egg, letting the excess drip back into the plate. Press the crumbs onto the sticks to help them adhere. Place the zucchini on a wire rack set over a baking sheet. Repeat until all the zucchini has been coated.

4. Pour 1 inch of oil into a deep fryer. Heat to 350°F. Fry the zucchini in batches, stirring to separate the pieces, for 2 minutes, or until golden. Drain on paper towels. Keep warm while frying the remaining zucchini. Serve hot.

Fried Parsley

This ever-popular fried herb is usually served as a garnish, but it can also be used to clarify oil after frying, and some people like to munch it as a vegetable. The parsley must be thoroughly dry, because once it hits the oil it will spatter slightly, so stand back. The safest way is to place the parsley in the fryer basket, cover the deep fryer, then slowly lower the basket into the hot oil.

MAKES 1 TO 1½ CUPS

1 large bunch of fresh parsley   Oil for frying

1. Remove the tough stems from the parsley. Rinse the parsley with cold water. Roll up the parsley in a clean kitchen towel or spin in a salad spinner until it is thoroughly dry.

2. Pour 1 inch of oil into a deep fryer. Heat to 375°F. Turn off the heat.

3. Place the parsley in the fryer basket. Close the fryer and slowly lower the basket into the hot oil. Fry 2 to 3 seconds, until the parsley turns a deep green and becomes crisp. Turn out onto paper towels. If you have an open fryer, use an oven mitt, avert your face, and stand back, because the parsley will "spit."

Suppli al Telefono

Whether you call them croquettes or Italian rice balls, this dish is so named because when the rice ball is pulled apart the melted cheese in the center strings out and by some stretch of the imagination looks like telephone wires. They can be served as an appetizer, first course, or side dish, or as an entrée topped with a light marinara sauce.

MAKES 15 RICE BALLS, 4 TO 6 SERVINGS

1½ cups chicken broth or water
½ teaspoon salt
¾ cup Arborio rice or long-grain white rice
2 tablespoons grated Parmesan cheese
4 ounces mozzarella cheese, cut into ½-inch cubes (about 1 cup)

2 eggs, separated
¼ cup chopped fresh parsley
2 ounces chopped prosciutto, smoked ham, or salami
¼ teaspoon pepper
½ cup unseasoned dry bread crumbs
Olive oil or other oil for frying

1. Place the broth and salt in a 1-quart saucepan. Stir in the rice. Bring to a boil; reduce the heat to low. Cover and simmer 15 minutes, or until the liquid is absorbed. Remove from the heat. Let stand 10 minutes. Stir in the Parmesan cheese and let cool.
2. Divide the mozzarella pieces into 15 equal piles, about 3 or 4 pieces each. Beat the egg yolks lightly and blend into the rice. Stir in the parsley, prosciutto, and pepper.
3. Divide the rice mixture into 15 equal mounds of about 2 tablespoons each. Slightly moisten your hands, then place a mound of rice in the palm of one hand. Make an indentation with the index finger of the other hand. Place the cubes of cheese from one pile in the indentation. Squeeze the hand together, shaping the rice mixture into

a small ball, about 1¾ inches in diameter, and enclosing the cheese completely. Repeat with the remaining rice and cheese.

4. In a pie plate, beat the egg whites until foamy with a fork. Place the bread crumbs on a sheet of wax paper. Gently roll the rice balls in the egg whites, then in the bread crumbs to coat completely. Place on a wire rack set over a baking sheet. Cover and refrigerate 1 hour.

5. Pour 1½ inches of oil into a deep fryer. Heat to 375°F. Fry 4 or 5 rice balls at a time 2½ to 3 minutes, until golden, turning once. Drain on paper towels. Keep warm while frying the remaining rice balls. Serve hot.

Pakoras

These herbed and spiced fritters from India will definitely become a favorite. The fritters take on interesting irregular shapes when fried. You can also serve them as an appetizer.

MAKES 4 TO 6 SERVINGS

1 teaspoon cumin seeds
1½ cups all-purpose flour
1 teaspoon salt
¼ teaspoon turmeric
¼ teaspoon cayenne
1 to 1¼ cups ice water
1 small cauliflower (1 pound)
1 tablespoon clarified butter or
  vegetable oil

½ cup minced scallions
1 garlic clove
1 large jalapeño pepper, seeded and
  minced
1 tablespoon minced fresh cilantro
Oil for frying
Cilantro Cream (page 32), optional

1. In a small skillet, toast the cumin seeds over low heat until crisp and fragrant, about 1 to 2 minutes. Let cool.
2. In a large bowl, combine the flour, salt, turmeric, cayenne, and the toasted cumin seeds. Whisk in enough of the ice water to make a thick batter. Let stand 30 minutes.
3. Trim the cauliflower and cut into 1-inch florets. There should be 3 to 3½ cups.
4. In a large skillet, heat the clarified butter or oil. Add the scallions, garlic, and jalapeño and cook over medium heat until soft, about 2 minutes. Stir in the cilantro. Stir into the batter. Add the cauliflower and stir to coat well.
5. Pour 1½ inches of oil into a deep fryer. Heat to 375°F. Gently drop the batter by heaping tablespoons into the hot oil, making sure each pakora contains a few pieces of cauliflower. Fry 4 to 5 at a time, until golden, about 3 minutes. Drain on paper towels. Serve warm with Cilantro Cream, if desired.

Corn Fritters

You can use fresh cut-off-the-cob corn kernels, frozen, or canned. To prepare fresh corn, stand the ear on end and cut the kernels from the cobs with a sharp knife. I like to serve these fritters with a drizzle of maple syrup.

MAKES 22 TO 24 FRITTERS, 4 TO 6 SERVINGS

1 cup all-purpose flour
1 teaspoon baking powder
1 teaspoon sugar
¾ teaspoon salt
¼ teaspoon white pepper
2 eggs, separated
½ cup milk

2 tablespoons butter, melted and
  slightly cooled
1½ cups fresh, frozen, or drained
  canned whole corn kernels
Oil for frying
Maple syrup (optional)

1. In a medium bowl, combine the flour, baking powder, sugar, salt, and pepper. Stir with a fork to mix. In a small bowl, beat the egg yolks with the milk and melted butter. Stir into the flour mixture just until combined. Stir in the corn. In a medium bowl, beat the egg whites until firm peaks form. Fold into the corn mixture until no streaks of white remain.

2. Pour 1½ inches of oil into a deep fryer. Heat to 375°F. Gently drop the batter by tablespoons, a few at a time, into the hot oil. A small ice cream scoop with a 1½-inch diameter is perfect for measuring out the batter. Fry 3 to 4 minutes, until golden, turning once. Drain on paper towels. Keep warm while frying the remaining fritters. Serve hot, drizzled with maple syrup, if desired.

Cornmeal-Coated Chiles Rellenos

These are a slightly different version of the classic chiles rellenos. They do take a little time to prepare, but the results are well worth the effort. Serve with a prepared enchilada sauce, or a combination of warmed Fresh Tomato Salsa (page 80) and cold Tomatillo Salsa (page 81).

MAKES 4 SERVINGS

8 medium to large poblano peppers, with stems
8 ounces Monterey Jack cheese with jalapeño peppers or Colby, jack, or cojack cheese
Oil for frying
1 cup sifted all-purpose flour, plus ⅓ cup for dredging
1 teaspoon baking powder
1 teaspoon salt
½ cup yellow cornmeal
2 eggs
1 cup milk
Enchilada sauce, Fresh Tomato Salsa (page 80), or Tomatillo Salsa (page 81)

1. Place the poblano peppers directly on the flames of a gas burner turned high or broil the chiles 3 inches from the heat source. Turn the peppers frequently, until they are roasted black and blistered. Let cool slightly, then place in a paper bag to steam 10 minutes.

2. Rub off as much of the charred skin from the chiles as possible. Make a slit from the stem end almost to the point of each pepper. Carefully remove the seeds and ribs, being careful not to break the pepper. Pat dry with paper towels.

3. Cut the cheese into 2¼ × ½ × ¼-inch sticks. Fill the peppers with equal amounts of the cheese and overlap the openings to close.

4. Pour 1½ inches of oil into a deep fryer. Heat to 375°F.

5. In a medium bowl, combine the 1 cup flour with the baking powder, and salt. Stir in the cornmeal. In a small bowl, beat the eggs until frothy. Blend in the milk. Pour into the cornmeal. Stir to combine to make a smooth, thick batter. Place the remaining ⅓ cup flour on wax paper.

6. Dredge the peppers thoroughly in the remaining ⅓ cup flour. Place 1 in the batter and spoon the batter over the pepper. Lift the pepper out by the stem, letting the excess batter drip back into the bowl. Carefully slide the pepper into the hot oil. Fry 2 at a time without crowding, 2 to 2½ minutes, until golden, turning once. Drain on paper towels. Keep warm. If the batter gets too thick, thin it out with a little bit of milk. Serve hot, with enchilada sauce, Fresh Tomato Salsa, or Tomatillo Salsa.

Fried Breads

Frying is the oldest form of bread cookery, and even today fried bread is a staple of the diet in many parts of the world. It is usually made with a grain, some salt, and just enough water added to make a dough that can be pinched off, rolled into thin rounds, or cut into squares or triangles before frying.

Results of these fry breads in the deep fryer are excellent. All of them cooked quickly and came out crisp and practically oil-free. Many can be reheated in the oven without losing their crispness, though practically all of them taste best the same day they are made.

Even though fried breads can be eaten plain as an accompaniment to the main course, many can also form a pocket for fillings. For example, the Navajo and Hopi Indians make a fry bread, to which I have added some savory herbs. While it is good plain, I top it with refried beans or a savory ground meat filling, like that used for tacos; then add all the trimmings—lettuce, tomatoes, cheese, guacamole, and sour cream—for what I call a Navajo taco. Fried breads can even be sweetened to turn them into a dessert.

Included in this chapter are American hush puppies, Indian pappadums and puris, and Mexican sopaipillas and tortillas. You can make your own tortilla chips or strips to top soups or to sprinkle over salads. Or use the deep fryer to fry up flour or corn tortillas in a basket shape to use as a container for salads or savory fillings. You will need a special tortilla basket fryer to make these, but they are readily available in different sizes in the cookware section of department stores or specialty cookware shops or through mail-order catalogs.

Hints and Tips

- Use large eggs in recipes that call for eggs.
- Keep breads covered with plastic wrap or wax paper to prevent drying out before and during frying.
- A small ice cream scoop with a 1½-inch diameter is helpful for measuring out the hush puppy batter. Hush puppies will get golden on the outside before they are done in the center. Try one as a test for doneness in the center by cutting open. The center should not be wet.
- In recipes that direct you to hold the bread in the oil with a metal spatula, begin counting the frying time from the time the bread rises to the surface.
- When making tortilla baskets, the cover of the deep fryer must remain open.
- Keep breads warm in a preheated 250°F. oven during the frying period.

Corn and Sage Hush Puppies

Legend has it that this deep-fried cornmeal dumpling was thrown by Southern cooks to hungry barking dogs to quiet them, calling, "Hush puppies." A small ice cream scoop, measuring 1½ inches in diameter (number 70), is perfect for scooping up the batter for frying. Hush puppies are a traditional accompaniment to fish, and for additional flavor, cook the hush puppies in the same oil in which you have fried the fish.

MAKES 28 TO 30 HUSH PUPPIES, 6 TO 8 SERVINGS

1½ cups stone-ground cornmeal,
  preferably white
½ cup all-purpose flour
1 tablespoon baking powder
1 teaspoon salt
1 teaspoon white pepper
1 teaspoon sugar
1 to 1¼ cups milk

1 egg
1 cup fresh, frozen, or canned whole
  corn kernels
½ cup chopped scallions
1 tablespoon chopped fresh sage leaves
  or 1 teaspoon crumbled dried
Corn oil or other vegetable oil for
  frying

1. In a large bowl, combine the cornmeal, flour, baking powder, salt, white pepper, and sugar. Mix with a fork. Make a well in the center.

2. In a medium bowl, beat 1 cup of milk and the egg until blended. Stir in the corn, scallions, and sage. Add all at once to the dry ingredients. Stir just to moisten. If the batter seems dry, add the remaining milk, 1 tablespoon at a time, until the mixture just holds together and is not runny.

3. Pour 1½ inches of oil into a deep fryer. Heat to 375°F. Using a small ice cream scoop or a 1-tablespoon measure, carefully drop 4 or 5 hush puppies into the hot oil. Fry 2½ to 3 minutes, turning once, until golden. Drain on paper towels. Keep warm while frying the remaining batter. Serve hot.

Bacon and Beer Hush Puppies

These hush puppies are my personal favorite. I like to serve them with steak, instead of a baked potato, and a huge green salad.

1½ cups stone-ground cornmeal, preferably white
½ cup all-purpose flour
2 teaspoons sugar
2 teaspoons baking powder
½ teaspoon baking soda
1 teaspoon salt
¾ to 1 teaspoon cayenne
½ cup buttermilk
1 egg
½ cup finely chopped onion
¼ cup crumbled crisp-cooked bacon
½ cup flat beer
Oil for frying

1. In a large bowl, combine the cornmeal, flour, sugar, baking powder, baking soda, salt, and cayenne. Mix with a fork. Make a well in the center.

2. In a medium bowl, whisk together the buttermilk, egg, and onion. Stir in the bacon, then the beer. Pour all at once into the cornmeal mixture. Stir just to moisten.

3. Pour 1½ inches of oil into a deep fryer. Heat to 375°F. Using a small ice cream scoop 1½ inches in diameter or a 1-tablespoon measure, carefully drop 4 or 5 hush puppies into the hot oil. Fry 2½ to 3 minutes, until golden, turning once. Drain on paper towels. Keep warm while frying the remaining batter. Serve hot.

Peppery Onion Hush Puppies

Once I started developing hush puppy recipes, I couldn't resist doing variations on a theme. White cornmeal is typically Southern, but yellow will yield equally good results.

MAKES 28 TO 30 HUSH PUPPIES, 6 TO 8 SERVINGS

1½ cups stone-ground cornmeal,
  preferably white
½ cup all-purpose flour
2 teaspoons sugar
2 teaspoons baking powder
1 teaspoon baking soda

1 teaspoon salt
1 teaspoon pepper
1¼ cups buttermilk
1 egg
½ cup finely chopped onion
Oil for frying

1. In a large bowl, combine the cornmeal, flour, sugar, baking powder, baking soda, salt, and pepper. Mix with a fork. Make a well in the center.

2. In a medium bowl, whisk together the buttermilk, egg, and onion. Pour all at once into the cornmeal mixture. Stir just to moisten.

3. Pour 1½ inches of oil into a deep fryer. Heat to 375°F. Using a small ice cream scoop 1½ inches in diameter or a 1-tablespoon measure, carefully drop 4 or 5 hush puppies into the hot oil. Fry 2½ to 3 minutes, turning once, until golden brown. Drain on paper towels. Keep warm while frying the remaining hush puppies. Serve hot.

Cumin-Flavored Cornmeal Chips

This recipe makes a lot of chips. Use them in place of tortilla chips for dipping into guacamole or salsa, or serve as a soup or chili accompaniment. The chips can be reheated in a low oven. Timesaving hint: Roll out all the dough into 5-inch rounds, then cut into wedges.

MAKES 128 CHIPS, 8 to 12 SERVINGS

3 cups buttermilk baking mix
¾ cup stone-ground yellow cornmeal,
   plus some for sprinkling
2 teaspoons ground cumin

¾ cup ice water
Corn oil or other vegetable oil for
   frying

1. In a large bowl, combine the baking mix, cornmeal, and cumin. Mix with a fork. Make a well in the center. Add the ice water and stir with the fork to make a soft dough. Divide the dough in half and shape each half into a flattened ball about 5 inches in diameter.

2. Cut each ball into 16 equal wedges; keep covered with a kitchen towel or plastic wrap to prevent drying out. Dust a work surface with cornmeal. Gather a wedge at a time and lightly shape into a ball, then roll out to a thin 5-inch round; the edges will be irregular. With a pastry wheel or sharp knife, cut each round into 4 triangles. Place on large baking sheets and keep covered. Repeat with the remaining dough.

3. Pour 1 inch of oil into a deep fryer. Heat to 375°F. Carefully slide 5 or 6 pieces of dough into the hot oil. Fry, turning, 20 seconds on each side, or until light golden and crisp. Drain on paper towels. The chips can be served warm or at room temperature. Store in an airtight container for up to 2 days.

Herbed Fry Bread

Usually attributed to the Navajo and Hopi Indians of the Southwest, this deep-fried bread is often featured at Indian festivals and country fairs. The Navajos would make a hole in the center of the flattened bread so they could lower it into the hot oil, usually lard, with a stick and then be able to raise it out of the oil when fried. I've added some hearty herbs.

MAKES 8 FRY BREADS

2 cups all-purpose flour
¼ cup powdered skim milk
2 teaspoons baking powder
½ teaspoon salt
1 tablespoon minced fresh rosemary or
   1 teaspoon dried crumbled

1 tablespoon minced fresh sage or
   1 teaspoon crumbled dried
2 tablespoons solid vegetable shortening
¾ cup ice water
Solid vegetable shortening, corn oil, or
   other vegetable oil for frying

1. In a large bowl, combine the flour, dry milk, baking powder, and salt. Mix with a fork. Stir in the rosemary and sage. Cut in the shortening with your fingers until the mixture is crumbly. Make a well in the center. Add the ice water and stir with a fork until the flour is thoroughly moistened. The dough will be sticky.

2. Turn out the dough onto a lightly floured surface and knead 3 to 4 minutes, until smooth. Cover with a bowl and let rest 30 minutes.

3. Divide the dough in half and shape each half into a ball. Cut each ball into 4 equal pieces. On a lightly floured surface, roll out each piece into a 5- to 6-inch round. If the dough gets too soft to roll out, place in the refrigerator for a few minutes. Make 3 (1-inch) cuts in the dough from the center to the edge, like spokes, spacing them evenly. Stack the rounds between sheets of wax paper and refrigerate 30 minutes.

4. Place enough shortening in small pieces in a deep fryer and melt, following the manufacturer's directions, to a depth of 1 inch or pour in 1 inch of oil. Heat to 375°F. Slip 1 pastry round at a time into the hot oil. When the bread rises to the top, gently press down with tongs. Fry 1½ to 2 minutes. Turn with tongs and fry another 1½ to 2 minutes, or until golden brown. Drain on paper towels.

TIP: Fry bread can be made up to 4 hours in advance. Let cool, then wrap securely in aluminum foil. Reheat in a preheated 325°F. oven for 10 to 12 minutes.

Pain Perdu with Mixed Berries

Pain perdu, literally translated from the French, means "lost bread." It is basically stale bread, fried. My grandmother Lena used to make a deep-fried Challah French toast, which was out of this world, so I've adapted both the French technique and my favorite grandmother's recipe and upscaled the presentation with mixed berries. It makes a great brunch dish.

MAKES 4 TO 6 SERVINGS

4 eggs
¾ cup heavy cream
¾ cup milk
¼ cup plus 1 tablespoon granulated
    sugar
1 teaspoon vanilla extract

1 teaspoon lemon or orange zest
6 slices of challah, French, or Italian
    bread, cut ¾ inch thick
4 cups mixed fresh berries
Oil for frying
Powdered sugar

1. In a large bowl, beat together the eggs, cream, milk, 1 tablespoon of the sugar, the vanilla, and the lemon or orange zest.

2. Place the bread in a lasagna pan or in a shallow baking dish large enough to hold the slices in a single layer. Pour the egg mixture over the bread; turn to coat the slices. Cover and refrigerate overnight.

3. About half an hour before you plan to serve the pain perdu, toss the berries with the remaining ¼ cup sugar. Let them stand at room temperature, tossing occasionally.

4. Pour 1 inch of oil into a deep fryer. Heat to 375°F. Using a wide metal spatula (a pancake turner will do), carefully slide 1 slice of bread into the hot oil. Fry 1½ minutes on each side. Lift out with a wide spatula and drain on paper towels. Keep warm while frying the remaining slices. Serve warm, with the mixed berries and a sprinkling of powdered sugar.

Puris

Puri is one of the many Indian flat breads that have become so popular recently. While whole wheat flour is traditional, this recipe uses a combination of whole wheat and all-purpose to give the bread a lighter texture. Reheat, if necessary, in a 350°F. oven for 3 to 5 minutes. Aerate the flours with a fork before measuring.

MAKES 8 PURIS

1 cup all-purpose flour

1 cup whole wheat flour

1 teaspoon salt

½ cup plus 1 tablespoon ice water

2 tablespoons vegetable oil

Oil for frying

1. In a large bowl, combine the all-purpose flour, whole wheat flour, and salt. Stir with a fork to mix. Drizzle the water over the flour. Mix with a fork until the dough is crumbly yet moist. If it is too dry, add more water 1 tablespoon at a time. The dough should be crumbly and slightly dry, *not wet.* Gather the dough into a ball and knead for about 10 minutes, until very stiff; do not skimp on the kneading time. Shape into a ball. Brush lightly with oil; cover with wax paper. Let stand 30 minutes at room temperature.

2. Cut the dough into 8 pieces. Shape each piece into a ball. Roll out each ball of dough on an unfloured surface to a 6½-inch round with slightly irregular edges. Keep the dough and rolled-out puris covered with plastic wrap to prevent drying out.

3. Pour 1 inch of oil into a deep fryer. Heat to 375°F. Slip 1 puri at a time into the hot oil. As the puri begins to rise, press down gently with a wide metal spatula to hold it under the oil a few seconds. The puris will begin to puff. Fry 1 minute on each side, until puffy and light brown. Drain on paper towels. Serve hot.

Cinnamon Snacks

Here's a great way to use up stale bread. It's a delightful snack that's particularly good with a cup of hot chocolate for kids of all ages.

MAKES 4 SERVINGS

4 cups (¾-inch) cubes of stale French or Italian bread
1 cup milk
1 egg
1 teaspoon vanilla extract

⅓ cup all-purpose flour
Oil for frying
Cinnamon Sugar (page 172), honey, or powdered sugar

1. Place the bread cubes in a single layer in an 8- or 9-inch square pan. In a medium bowl, whisk together the milk, egg, and vanilla. Pour over the bread cubes; turn them to coat. Let stand at room temperature, turning once or twice, until the bread absorbs the liquid.

2. Place the bread cubes on paper towels and pat to remove the excess liquid. Place the flour in a large plastic food storage bag. Add the bread cubes, a handful at a time, and shake gently to coat. Place the cubes on a wire rack set over a baking sheet.

3. Pour 1 inch of oil into a deep fryer. Heat to 375°F. Fry the bread cubes in batches without crowding, turning occasionally, 2 to 2½ minutes per batch, until light golden brown. Drain on paper towels. Serve warm or at room temperature. Sprinkle with Cinnamon Sugar, drizzle with warm honey, or dust with powdered sugar.

Pappadums

Often served as an accompaniment to curries, these round, paper-thin wafers are usually flame-toasted in India until crisp. This version is fried, and the flavor is heightened with pepper. The recipe can be halved, if desired. Reheat, if necessary, in a 475°F. oven for 3 to 5 minutes.

MAKES 2 DOZEN PAPPADUMS

1¼ cups all-purpose flour
1¼ cups whole wheat flour
1 teaspoon salt

1 teaspoon cracked black pepper
1 cup ice water
Oil for frying

1. In a large bowl, combine the all-purpose flour, whole wheat flour, salt, and pepper. Stir with a fork to mix. Make a well in the center. Add the ice water and stir with the fork to combine. If the mixture seems dry, gradually add additional water, 1 tablespoon at a time, just until the dough clings together but is not sticky.

2. Turn out the dough onto a lightly floured surface and knead for 5 minutes. Form into a ball. Cut into quarters, then cut each quarter into 6 equal pieces. Form each piece of dough into a ball by cupping the palm of your hand and rolling the dough in a circle on an unfloured surface. Cover the pieces with a bowl and let rest 30 minutes.

3. On a lightly floured surface, roll out each ball into a paper-thin round 6 inches in diameter. Place in a single layer on large baking sheets. Do not stack, or the pappadums will stick to each other. Cover with wax paper.

4. Pour 1 inch of oil into a deep fryer. Heat to 375°F. Slide 1 pappadum at a time into the hot oil; it will sink and then float to the top. When the pappadum rises to the surface, tap it down with tongs and gently push under the oil; at this point it will puff. Fry 15 to 20 seconds on each side, until puffed and light golden. Drain on paper towels.

Sopaipillas

Pronounced "soh-pie-PEEL-yah," these little pillows are usually triangular. Most often they are broken open, spread with butter and drizzled with honey, and served at breakfast, or rolled in cinnamon sugar, topped with whipped cream, and served with fruit. They can also be made into larger shapes, which can be cut open and filled with a bean or meat mixture like a Greek pocket bread. Reheat, if necessary, in a 350°F. oven for 3 to 5 minutes.

MAKES 8 SOPAIPILLAS

1 cup all-purpose flour
1½ teaspoons baking powder
¼ teaspoon salt
2 tablespoons butter-flavored
   shortening, regular vegetable shortening, or lard

6 tablespoons warm water
Oil for frying

1. In a large bowl, combine the flour, baking powder, and salt. Stir with a fork to mix. Cut in the shortening with a pastry blender until the mixture is crumbly. Add the water all at once. Stir lightly with the fork until the mixture is just combined.

2. Turn the dough out onto a well-floured board and gently knead 8 to 10 times. The dough should be soft but not sticky. Cover the dough with a bowl. Let rest at room temperature for 15 minutes.

3. Divide the dough in half; keep the other half covered with wax paper to prevent drying out. On a lightly floured surface, roll out the dough to a 10 × 5-inch rectangle (a ruler helps). With a fluted pastry cutter or a knife, cut the dough into two 5-inch squares, than cut each square diagonally in half into 2 triangles. Repeat with the remaining dough.

4. Pour 1½ inches of oil into a deep fryer. Heat to 375°F. Slide 1 sopaipilla at a time into the hot oil. As the dough starts to rise but does not break the surface of the oil, hold it down under the oil with a potato masher or a wide slotted metal spatula until you feel the sopaipilla begin to strain against the potato masher or spatula; it will begin to puff. As the sopaipilla begins to puff, release it and fry until golden brown, about 2 minutes. Turn the sopaipilla over with the spatula and fry 1 minute longer, or until golden brown on the second side. Lift out with a slotted metal spoon. Drain on paper towels. Repeat the procedure with the remaining dough. You can fry 2 sopaipillas at a time; add the second one after the first has been released. Serve warm.

Corn Tortilla Chips

You can make your own tortilla chips at a fraction of what they cost in the bag. Serve as dippers for guacamole or to eat with chili. Cut into strips, they can be used to garnish soups or salads. If necessary, chips can be reheated in a 300°F. oven for 3 to 5 minutes.

Oil for frying
1 (10-ounce) package corn tortillas,
   6 inches in diameter
1 teaspoon salt

¼ teaspoon ground cumin
¼ teaspoon chili powder
¼ teaspoon pepper

1. Pour 1½ inches of oil into a deep fryer. Heat to 375°F.

2. Cut each tortilla in half, then cut each half into 3 wedges or into ¼-inch strips. Fry in batches without crowding, turning, until crisp and golden, 1 to 2 minutes. Drain on paper towels.

3. In a small cup, combine the salt, cumin, chili powder, and pepper. Sprinkle lightly over the chips or strips while they are still warm.

Tortilla Baskets

Tortilla fryer baskets can be purchased in the cookware section of department stores, in specialty cookware shops, or by mail order. Serve these edible baskets as containers for chili or main-dish salads; or sprinkle with cinnamon and sugar while warm, then fill with fresh fruit or ice cream and top with a fruit sauce or a chocolate syrup. This recipe will not work in a slope-sided deep fryer. Remove the wire basket of the deep fryer and keep the lid open during frying.

MAKES 6 TORTILLA BASKETS

Oil for frying   6 (8-inch) flour or corn tortillas

1. Pour 2 inches of oil into a deep fryer. Heat to 375°F. Dip the tortilla basket fryer into the hot oil and drain on paper towels; this is to prevent the tortilla from sticking.
2. Place 1 flour or corn tortilla into the larger wire basket of the tortilla fryer. Place the smaller wire basket on top of the tortilla. Fasten the handles together with the clip provided.
3. Gently lower the tortilla basket fryer into the hot oil. Fry the tortilla until crisp and golden, 1 to 2 minutes. Remove the basket from the oil and place on paper towels. Remove the clip; carefully remove the smaller wire basket and turn the fried tortilla "basket" out onto paper towels to drain. Repeat with the remaining tortillas.

NOTE: Use the pliable tortillas found in the refrigerator case. If the tortillas seem dry, follow the manufacturer's directions for softening.

Doughnuts

The deep fryer is the quintessential machine for making yeast-raised, cake-style, or cream puff-dough doughnuts. Besides, who can resist a fresh warm doughnut dripping with glaze, dusted with sugar, and topped with nuts, sprinkles, or coconut? There are as many variations as there are tastes—round, square, rectangular, or strips, plain or frosted, jelly-filled or chocolate. You won't even have to visit a doughnut shop to get a batch when your deep fryer can turn out all the doughnuts you want right in your own kitchen!

The first American doughnuts, sometimes spelled donuts, did not have holes in their centers, but were literally plain dough, fried, and called cakes. Some give credit to a nineteenth-century Maine sea captain, or so the story goes, who had his fill of his wife's (mother's) soggy-centered fried cakes and testily instructed her to cut out the middle where it wasn't cooked. Another popular story features a Nauset Indian who playfully shot an arrow into one of his wife's friend's cakes. In fright she dropped the ring of dough in a kettle of hot fat. Today, the hole is as popular as the ring.

The dough for cake doughnuts is soft and it helps greatly if the dough is chilled. Roll out and cut the dough when you are just ready to fry so that it will not warm up too much. The best temperature for deep-frying doughnuts is 375°F. Use a large metal spatula that has been dipped in the hot oil first to prevent sticking and gently slide the doughnut into the hot fat. This technique also helps the doughnut keep its shape better. As the doughnuts rise to the top of the fat, turn them over, using a slotted metal spoon. This helps to prevent cracking, especially common with cake doughnuts. Try not to puncture the doughnuts while frying as this allows more oil absorption and you may wind up with "sinkers"—those heavy doughnuts we have all eaten at one time or another.

Bismarcks are yeast-raised doughnuts that have a filling in the center; the most popular is the jelly doughnut. Crullers and beignets are made with a *choux* paste, the same dough that is used to make cream puffs. Doughnuts should be glazed while slightly warm, or dusted with cinnamon sugar made with either powdered or granulated sugar. They are also best eaten the same day they are made.

Hints and Tips

- Aerate the flour before sifting in recipes that call for sifted flour.
- Use large eggs.
- Glazes are interchangeable and can be used with any doughnut to suit your taste.

Cake Doughnuts

No need to go to a doughnut shop when you can make these fine-textured, nutmeg-flavored doughnuts at home.

MAKES 2 DOZEN DOUGHNUTS AND DOUGHNUT HOLES

4 cups sifted all-purpose flour
4 teaspoons baking powder
½ teaspoon salt
1½ teaspoons grated nutmeg or mace
¼ cup solid vegetable shortening
¾ cup sugar

2 eggs
1 teaspoon vanilla extract
¾ cup milk
Vegetable oil for frying
Vanilla Glaze (recipe follows)

1. In a medium bowl, combine the flour, baking powder, salt, and nutmeg. Mix with a fork.

2. In a large bowl, beat the shortening and the sugar with an electric mixer on medium speed, until crumbly. Add the eggs and vanilla; beat until blended. Beat in the milk. Beat in 1 cup of the flour mixture until well mixed. Stir in the remaining flour mixture with a wooden spoon until a soft, slightly sticky dough forms. Cover the bowl with plastic wrap and refrigerate the dough at least 4 hours or overnight.

3. On a floured surface, roll out the dough ⅜ inch thick. Cut out doughnuts with a floured 2¾-inch doughnut cutter. Place the doughnuts and doughnut holes on large baking sheets. Reroll the trimmings and cut out more doughnuts. Place the baking sheets in the refrigerator while heating the oil.

4. Pour 1½ inches of oil into a deep fryer. Heat to 375°F. Lifting the doughnuts with a wide slotted metal spatula, lower 2 or 3 at a time into the hot oil. As the doughnuts rise to the surface, turn them over. Fry the doughnuts and doughnut holes 1 to 1½ minutes on each side, until golden brown. Drain on paper towels. Dip the tops of the warm doughnuts in the Vanilla Glaze. Let stand on a wire rack to set the glaze.

Vanilla Glaze

MAKES 1⅓ CUPS, ENOUGH TO GLAZE 2 DOZEN DOUGHNUTS AND DOUGHNUT HOLES

3 cups powdered sugar
3 to 4 tablespoons milk

1 teaspoon vanilla extract

In a medium bowl, whisk together the ingredients until smooth and of glaze consistency.

Lemon Buttermilk Doughnuts

4¼ cups sifted all-purpose flour

2 teaspoons baking powder

1 teaspoon baking soda

½ teaspoon salt

¼ teaspoon grated nutmeg or mace

2 eggs

1 cup sugar

3 tablespoons unsalted butter, softened

1 tablespoon grated lemon zest

1 cup buttermilk

Vegetable oil for frying

Lemon Glaze (recipe follows)

1. In a medium bowl, combine the flour, baking powder, baking soda, salt, and nutmeg. Mix with a fork.

2. In a large bowl, beat the eggs, sugar, and butter with an electric mixer on medium speed, until creamy. Add the lemon zest. On low speed, beat in the flour mixture alternately with the buttermilk in thirds, beginning and ending with the flour mixture. Cover the bowl with plastic wrap and refrigerate the dough at least 4 hours or overnight.

3. On a floured surface, roll out the dough ⅜ inch thick. Cut out doughnuts with a floured 2¾-inch doughnut cutter. Place the doughnuts and doughnut holes on large baking sheets. Reroll the trimmings and cut out more doughnuts. Place the baking sheets in the refrigerator while heating the oil.

4. Pour 1½ inches of oil into a deep fryer. Heat to 375°F. Lifting the doughnuts with a wide slotted metal spatula, lower 2 or 3 at a time into the hot oil. As the doughnuts rise to the surface, turn them over. Fry the doughnuts and doughnut holes 1 to 2 minutes on each side, until golden brown. Drain on paper towels. Dip the tops of the warm doughnuts in the Lemon Glaze. Let stand on a wire rack to set the glaze.

Lemon Glaze

MAKES 1⅓ CUPS, OR ENOUGH TO GLAZE 2 DOZEN DOUGHNUTS AND DOUGHNUT HOLES

3 cups powdered sugar
1½ teaspoons grated lemon zest

1½ tablespoons fresh lemon juice
2 to 3 tablespoons water

In a medium bowl, combine the powdered sugar, lemon zest, and lemon juice. Whisk in the water until smooth and of glaze consistency.

Orange Crullers

Crullers could be described as doughnuts with a French connection. Made with the same pastry that is used to make cream puffs for profiteroles, *they puff up when fried and become light and airy.*

MAKES 12 CRULLERS

1 cup water
¼ cup solid vegetable shortening
2 tablespoons granulated sugar
½ teaspoon salt
1¼ cups sifted all-purpose flour

4 eggs
1 teaspoon grated orange zest
Oil for frying
½ recipe Orange Glaze (recipe follows)
  or powdered sugar

1. Cut out 12 (4-inch) squares of aluminum foil. Generously grease one side of each foil square with vegetable shortening. Press a 2½-inch round biscuit cutter into the center of each foil square to mark a circle. This is to give you a guide when shaping the crullers. Place the foil pieces on large baking sheets.

2. In a 3-quart saucepan, combine the water, shortening, sugar, and salt. Bring to a full rolling boil over high heat, stirring occasionally, to melt the shortening. Quickly add the flour all at once. Beat vigorously with a wooden spoon until the dough leaves the sides of the pan and forms a ball, about 1 minute. Remove from the heat.

3. Make a well in the center of the dough ball. Add the eggs, 1 at a time, beating well after each addition, until the pastry is smooth, shiny, and satiny. Beat in the orange zest.

4. Fit a large pastry bag with a large star-tip tube (½-inch diameter); fill with dough. Press the dough onto the greased foil to form rings about 2½ inches in diameter, overlapping the ends of the rings slightly. Set the baking sheets in the refrigerator and chill the dough for 15 minutes.

5. Pour 1½ inches of oil into a deep fryer. Heat to 370°F. Carefully slide 2 or 3 crullers, foil-side up, into the hot oil. As the crullers rise to the top of the oil, turn them over. Lift out the foil with a slotted spoon and discard. Fry the crullers 5 minutes, turning once or twice, until they are light golden brown and puffed. Remove with a slotted spoon. Drain on paper towels. Repeat with the remaining crullers.

6. When the crullers are slightly cool, dip the tops into the Orange Glaze, letting the excess drip back into the bowl. Let stand on a wire rack until the glaze sets. Or simply dust the crullers with powdered sugar while still slightly warm.

Orange Glaze

3 cups powdered sugar
1 teaspoon grated orange zest

3 to 4 tablespoons orange juice

In a medium bowl, whisk together all the ingredients until smooth and of glaze consistency.

Banana Spice Doughnuts

Bananas, sour cream, and spices make for a flavorful doughnut. Use overripe bananas—the riper the bananas, the stronger the banana flavor in the doughnut.

MAKES 2 DOZEN DOUGHNUTS AND DOUGHNUT HOLES

4 cups sifted all-purpose flour
5 teaspoons baking powder
½ teaspoon baking soda
½ teaspoon salt
1½ teaspoons ground cinnamon
¾ teaspoon grated nutmeg
¾ teaspoon ground cloves
¼ cup solid vegetable shortening

¾ cup granulated sugar
2 eggs
1 cup overripe mashed bananas (2 to 3 medium)
⅓ cup sour cream
Vegetable oil for frying
Powdered sugar or glaze of your choice

1. In a medium bowl, combine the flour, baking powder, baking soda, salt, cinnamon, nutmeg, and cloves. Mix with a fork.

2. In a large bowl, beat the shortening and the sugar with an electric mixer at medium speed until crumbly. Add the eggs; beat to combine. Blend in the bananas and the sour cream. Beat in 1 cup of the flour mixture. Stir in the remaining flour mixture with a wooden spoon until the mixture forms a soft, slightly sticky dough. Cover the bowl with plastic wrap and refrigerate the dough at least 4 hours or overnight.

3. On a floured surface, roll out the dough ⅜ inch thick. Cut out doughnuts with a floured 2¾-inch doughnut cutter. Place the doughnuts and doughnut holes on large baking sheets. Reroll the trimmings and cut out more doughnuts. Place the baking sheets in the refrigerator while heating the oil.

4. Pour 1½ inches of oil into a deep fryer. Heat to 375°F. Lifting the doughnuts with a wide slotted metal spatula, lower 2 or 3 at a time into the hot oil. As the doughnuts rise to the surface, turn them over. Fry 2 or 3 doughnuts or 4 or 5 doughnut holes for 1 to 1½ minutes on each side, until golden brown. Drain on paper towels. Dust with powdered sugar or glaze while still warm.

Chocolate-Sour Cream Doughnuts

2 (1-ounce) squares unsweetened
   chocolate, coarsely chopped
1 tablespoon solid vegetable shortening
3¾ cups sifted all-purpose flour
2 teaspoons baking powder
1 teaspoon baking soda
1 teaspoon salt
1 teaspoon ground cinnamon

1¼ cups sugar
3 eggs
1 teaspoon vanilla extract
1 cup sour cream
Oil for frying
Chocolate Glaze (recipe follows)
Chopped walnuts (optional)

1. In a small skillet, melt the chocolate with the shortening over low heat, stirring constantly, until the chocolate is melted. Mix well. Remove from the heat and let cool.

2. In a medium bowl, combine the flour, baking powder, baking soda, salt, and cinnamon. Stir with a fork to mix well.

3. In the large bowl of an electric mixer, beat the sugar, eggs, and vanilla on medium speed until well mixed. Beat in the melted chocolate and shortening. Add the flour mixture alternately with the sour cream, mixing just until combined. You may have to use a wooden spoon to blend in the last of the flour. Cover the bowl with plastic wrap and refrigerate the dough at least 2 hours.

4. On a floured surface, roll out the dough ⅜ inch thick. Cut out doughnuts with a floured 2¾-inch doughnut cutter. Place the doughnuts and doughnut holes on large baking sheets. Reroll the trimmings and cut out more doughnuts. Place the baking sheets in the refrigerator while heating the oil.

5. Pour 1½ inches of oil into a deep fryer. Heat to 375°F. Lifting the doughnuts with a wide slotted metal spatula, lower 2 or 3 at a time into the hot oil. As the doughnuts rise to the surface, turn them over. Fry the doughnuts and doughnut holes 1 or 2 minutes on each side, until a deeper brown and cooked through. Drain on paper towels. Glaze with Chocolate Glaze while still warm and dip into chopped walnuts, if you like.

Chocolate Glaze

3 tablespoons unsalted butter, softened
3 (1-ounce) squares unsweetened
   chocolate, cut up

3 cups powdered sugar
1 teaspoon vanilla extract
6 to 7 tablespoons very hot tap water

In a heavy medium saucepan, melt the butter with the chocolate over low heat, stirring constantly, until the chocolate is melted. Remove from the heat. Whisk in the sugar, vanilla, and enough of the hot water so that the mixture is smooth and of glaze consistency.

Beignets

Beignets, *French for "fritters," are a traditional New Orleans treat, usually served for breakfast or as an afternoon snack with café au lait (coffee with milk) or café noir (black).*

MAKES 22 TO 24

1 cup water

8 tablespoons (1 stick) butter

1 tablespoon granulated sugar

¼ teaspoon salt

1 cup sifted all-purpose flour

4 eggs

1 teaspoon vanilla extract

Oil for frying

Powdered sugar

1. In a 3-quart saucepan, combine the water, butter, sugar, and salt. Bring to a full rolling boil over high heat, stirring occasionally to melt the butter. Quickly add the flour all at once. Beat vigorously with a wooden spoon until the dough leaves the sides of the pan and forms a ball, about 1 minute.

2. Make a well in the center of the dough. Add the eggs, 1 at a time, beating well after each addition until the pastry is smooth, shiny, and satiny. Beat in the vanilla.

3. Pour 1½ inches of oil into a deep fryer. Heat to 375°F. Drop the batter by heaping rounded teaspoonfuls into the hot oil. Fry 3 or 4 at a time, until puffed and golden brown, about 5 minutes, turning occasionally. Drain on paper towels. Dust with powdered sugar while still warm. Serve warm.

Old-Fashioned Cinnamon Doughnuts

Unlike most yeast doughs, this one requires no kneading. The recipe yields a light and tender round doughnut.

MAKES 12 TO 14 DOUGHNUTS

1 (¼-ounce) envelope active dry yeast
1 cup warm milk (105° to 115°F.)
⅓ cup sugar
3½ cups all-purpose flour
¾ teaspoon salt
½ teaspoon grated nutmeg

5 tablespoons plus 1 teaspoon butter
  (⅓ cup), melted
2 eggs, lightly beaten
Oil for frying
Cinnamon Sugar (recipe follows)

1. In a small bowl, sprinkle the yeast over the warm milk. Add a pinch of sugar and stir to combine.

2. In a large bowl, combine the flour, remaining sugar, salt, and nutmeg. Mix with a fork. Add the dissolved yeast mixture, melted butter, and eggs. Stir just until blended. The dough will be slightly sticky and rough looking in appearance. Cover the bowl with plastic wrap and let the dough rise in a warm place away from drafts until double in volume, about 1 hour.

3. Turn out the dough onto a well-floured surface and toss lightly until the dough is no longer sticky. Roll out the dough ½ inch thick. Cut out doughnuts with a floured 3-inch round cutter. Place the doughnuts on a large baking sheet. Reroll the trimmings lightly and cut out to make more doughnuts. Cover the doughnuts with wax paper and let rise until double in volume, about 20 minutes.

4. Pour 1½ inches of oil into a deep fryer. Heat to 375°F. Lifting the doughnuts with a wide slotted metal spatula, lower 2 or 3 at a time into the hot oil. Fry the doughnuts 2 to 2½ minutes, until light golden brown, turning once. Drain on paper towels. Coat with Cinnamon Sugar while slightly warm.

Cinnamon Sugar

1 cup granulated sugar

4 teaspoons ground cinnamon

In a small bowl, stir together the sugar and cinnamon. Place in a plastic bag for ease of coating doughnuts.

Churros

Churros are Mexican crullers. The hint of orange, lemon, or lime peel to flavor the oil is traditional.

MAKES 16 CHURROS

Oil for frying
Wide strips of zest from ½ lime,
    lemon, or orange
1 cup water
1 tablespoon granulated sugar

½ teaspoon salt
1 cup all-purpose flour
2 eggs
Powdered or granulated sugar or Cinna-
    mon Sugar (page 172)

1. Pour 1½ inches of oil into a deep fryer. Add the citrus zest—colored part of the peel only, no white—to the oil. Heat to 375°F. When the temperature is reached, remove and discard the peel with a slotted spoon.

2. In a medium saucepan, combine the water, sugar, and salt. Bring to a full rolling boil over high heat. Quickly add the flour all at once and beat vigorously with a wooden spoon until the dough forms a ball and leaves the sides of the pan, about 1 minute. Remove from the heat.

3. Make a well in the center of the dough. Add the eggs, 1 at a time, beating well after each addition until the dough is smooth, shiny, and satiny.

4. Spoon the dough into a large pastry bag filled with a large star-tip tube (number 6). Force the dough through the pastry tube into 4-inch lengths. Snip the dough off with scissors and let drop into the hot oil. Fry 3 or 4 churros at a time, until golden brown, 3 to 4 minutes, turning once. Drain on paper towels. Dust with sugar while still warm. Serve warm.

Jelly Doughnuts

Any doughnut with a filling inside is called a Bismarck. The most well known is the jelly doughnut.

1 (¼-ounce) envelope active dry yeast
1 cup warm milk (105° to 115°F.)
⅓ cup granulated sugar
3½ cups all-purpose flour
¾ teaspoon salt
½ teaspoon grated nutmeg
5 tablespoons plus 1 teaspoon butter
   (⅓ cup), melted

2 eggs, lightly beaten
Oil for frying
½ to ⅔ cup raspberry preserves or red
   currant jelly
Granulated or powdered sugar

1. In a small bowl, sprinkle the yeast over the warm milk. Add a pinch of sugar and stir to mix.

2. In a large bowl, combine the flour, remaining sugar, salt, and nutmeg. Mix with a fork. Add the dissolved yeast mixture, melted butter, and eggs. Stir just until blended. The dough will be slightly sticky and rough looking. Cover the bowl with plastic wrap and let the dough rise in a warm place away from drafts until double in volume, about 1 hour.

3. Turn out the dough onto a well-floured surface and toss lightly until the dough is no longer sticky. Roll out the dough ½ inch thick. Cut out doughnuts with a floured 3-inch round cutter. Place the doughnuts on a large baking sheet. Reroll the trimmings lightly to make more doughnuts. Cover the doughnuts with wax paper and let rise until double in volume, about 20 minutes.

4. Pour 1½ inches of oil into a deep fryer. Heat to 375°F. Lift the doughnuts with a wide slotted metal spatula. Lower 2 or 3 doughnuts at a time into the hot oil. Fry 2 to 2½ minutes, until golden brown, turning once. Drain on paper towels.

5. With a small knife, make a deep slit about 1 inch long on the side of each doughnut. Using a small spoon, fill with 2 teaspoons of the raspberry preserves, or fit a pastry bag with a small plain tube and fill each doughnut. Gently squeeze the cut edges together to close the doughnut. Coat with granulated sugar or dust with powdered sugar.

Spiced Pumpkin Doughnuts

4 cups sifted all-purpose flour
2 teaspoons baking powder
1 teaspoon baking soda
1 teaspoon salt
1½ teaspoons ground cinnamon
½ teaspoon grated nutmeg
½ teaspoon ground ginger
¼ teaspoon ground cloves

1¼ cups granulated sugar
2 eggs
1 cup canned solid pack pumpkin (not pumpkin pie filling)
⅔ cup buttermilk
2 tablespoons butter, melted
Oil for frying
Granulated or powdered sugar

1. In a medium bowl, combine the flour, baking powder, baking soda, salt, cinnamon, nutmeg, ginger, and cloves. Mix with a fork.

2. In a large bowl with an electric mixer on medium speed, beat the sugar with the eggs until light and fluffy. On low speed, beat in the pumpkin, buttermilk, and melted butter until blended. Stir in the flour mixture until combined. Cover the bowl with plastic wrap and refrigerate 3 hours or longer.

3. On a lightly floured surface with floured hands or a floured rolling pin, pat or roll out the dough ¾ inch thick. Cut out doughnuts with a floured 2¾-inch cutter. Place the doughnuts and doughnut holes on large baking sheets. Reroll the trimmings and cut out more doughnuts. Place the baking sheets in the refrigerator while heating the oil.

4. Pour 1½ inches of oil into a deep fryer. Heat to 375°F. Lifting the doughnuts with a wide slotted metal spatula, lower 2 or 3 at a time into the hot oil. As the doughnuts rise to the surface, turn them over. Fry the doughnuts and doughnut holes 1½ to 2 minutes on each side, until golden brown. Drain on paper towels. Serve plain or dusted with granulated or powdered sugar.

Walnut Puffs

This easy drop doughnut resembles the hole without the ring.

MAKES 2 DOZEN WALNUT PUFFS

Oil for frying
2 cups all-purpose flour
¼ cup granulated sugar
1 tablespoon baking powder
½ teaspoon salt
½ teaspoon ground cinnamon
½ teaspoon grated nutmeg

1 egg
½ cup milk
½ cup vegetable oil
¼ cup orange juice
½ cup coarsely chopped walnuts
Powdered sugar

1. Pour 1½ inches of oil into a deep fryer. Heat to 365°F.

2. In a large bowl, combine the flour, sugar, baking powder, salt, cinnamon, and nutmeg. Mix with a fork.

3. In a medium bowl, beat the egg lightly. Beat in the milk, oil, and orange juice until combined. Add to the flour mixture with the walnuts. Stir just to moisten.

4. Carefully drop the dough into the hot oil by heaping teaspoonfuls. Fry 5 or 6 at a time for 3 minutes, turning once, until golden brown. Drain on paper towels. Dust with powdered sugar while still warm.

Carrot Cake Doughnuts

To make chopping easier, sprinkle the raisins with a little flour so they don't stick to the knife.

MAKES 2 DOZEN DOUGHNUTS AND DOUGHNUT HOLES

4 cups sifted all-purpose flour
5 teaspoons baking powder
1 teaspoon salt
1 teaspoon ground cinnamon
½ teaspoon grated nutmeg
¼ cup solid vegetable shortening
¾ cup sugar
2 eggs

¾ cup milk
1 teaspoon vanilla extract
1½ cups shredded carrots (about
   3 medium)
½ cup chopped golden raisins
Oil for frying
Honey Glaze (recipe follows)
Flaked coconut (optional)

1. In a small bowl, combine the flour, baking powder, salt, cinnamon, and nutmeg. Mix with a fork.

2. In a large bowl, beat the shortening and sugar with an electric mixer on medium speed until crumbly. Beat in the eggs, milk, and vanilla until combined. Beat in 1 cup of the flour mixture until blended. Stir in the carrots and raisins. Stir in the remaining flour with a wooden spoon until the mixture forms a soft, slightly sticky dough. Cover the bowl with plastic wrap and refrigerate the dough at least 4 hours or overnight.

3. On a floured surface, roll out the dough ⅜ inch thick. Cut out doughnuts with a floured 2¾-inch doughnut cutter. Place the doughnuts and holes on large baking sheets. Reroll the trimmings and cut out more doughnuts. Place the baking sheets in the refrigerator while heating the oil.

4. Pour 1½ inches of oil into a deep fryer. Heat to 375°F. Lifting the doughnuts with a wide slotted metal spatula, lower 2 or 3 at a time into the hot oil. As the doughnuts rise to the surface, turn them over. Fry the doughnuts and doughnut holes 1½ minutes on each side, until golden brown. Drain on paper towels. Glaze with Honey Glaze while still warm. Dip in coconut, if desired. Let stand on a wire rack until the glaze sets before serving.

Honey Glaze

MAKES 1½ CUPS, ENOUGH TO GLAZE 2 DOZEN DOUGHNUTS AND DOUGHNUT HOLES

¾ cup honey
3 cups sifted powdered sugar

1 to 2 tablespoons water

In a small saucepan, heat the honey over medium-low heat just to boiling. Remove from the heat and beat in the sugar and water until smooth and of glaze consistency.

Zucchini Cake Doughnuts

After shredding, the zucchini must be drained of excess liquid, otherwise the dough will be too soft to work with.

MAKES 2 DOZEN DOUGHNUTS AND DOUGHNUT HOLES

4 cups sifted all-purpose flour
5 teaspoons baking powder
1 teaspoon salt
¼ cup solid vegetable shortening
¾ cup sugar
2 eggs
¾ cup milk

1½ teaspoons grated lemon zest
1 teaspoon vanilla extract
1¼ cups shredded zucchini, drained
½ cup finely chopped walnuts
Oil for frying
Lemon Glaze (page 163)

1. In a medium bowl, combine the flour, baking powder, and salt. Mix with a fork.
2. In a large bowl, beat the shortening and the sugar with an electric mixer on medium speed, until crumbly. Beat in the eggs, milk, lemon zest, and vanilla until combined. Beat in 1 cup of the flour mixture until blended. Stir in the zucchini and walnuts. Stir in the remaining flour with a wooden spoon until the mixture forms a soft, slightly sticky dough. Cover the bowl with plastic wrap and refrigerate the dough at least 4 hours or overnight.
3. On a floured surface, roll out the dough ⅜ inch thick. Cut out doughnuts with a floured 2¾-inch doughnut cutter. Place the doughnuts and holes on large baking sheets. Reroll the trimmings and cut out more doughnuts. Place the baking sheets in the refrigerator while heating the oil.
4. Pour 1½ inches of oil into a deep fryer. Heat to 375°F. Lifting the doughnuts with a wide slotted metal spatula, lower 2 or 3 at a time into the hot oil. As the doughnuts rise to the surface, turn them over. Fry the doughnuts and doughnut holes 1½ minutes on each side, until golden brown. Drain on paper towels. Glaze with Lemon Glaze while still warm. Let stand on a wire rack until the glaze sets before serving.

Potato Doughnuts

Yeast-raised doughnuts made with mashed potatoes are exceptionally tender. Be sure to begin a day ahead. One-fourth pound of potatoes will yield 1 cup mashed potatoes.

MAKES 2 DOZEN DOUGHNUTS AND DOUGHNUT HOLES

1 (¼-ounce) envelope active dry yeast
1½ cups warm water (105° to 115°F.)
⅔ cup granulated sugar
1½ teaspoons salt
1 teaspoon grated nutmeg
⅔ cup solid vegetable shortening
2 eggs

1 cup unseasoned lukewarm mashed
 potatoes
6 to 7 cups all-purpose flour
Oil for frying
Powdered or granulated sugar or glaze
 of your choice (optional)

1. In a large bowl, sprinkle the yeast over the warm water. Add a pinch of sugar and stir to mix. Let stand 5 minutes, until foamy. Stir in the remaining sugar, salt, nutmeg, shortening, eggs, potatoes, and 3 cups of the flour. Beat until smooth. Mix in enough of the remaining flour to make a soft dough.

2. Turn the dough out onto a lightly floured surface. Knead until smooth and elastic, about 5 minutes. Place in a large greased bowl; turn over to coat both sides. Cover with plastic wrap and refrigerate overnight.

3. The next day, punch the dough down. Turn out onto a lightly floured surface and knead a few times to get out any large air bubbles. Roll out the dough ½ inch thick. Cut out doughnuts with a floured 2¾-inch doughnut cutter. Place on large baking sheets. Cover and let rise until double in volume, about 45 to 60 minutes.

4. Pour 1½ inches of oil into a deep fryer. Heat to 375°F. Lifting the doughnuts with a wide slotted metal spatula, lower 2 or 3 at a time into the hot oil. Fry the doughnuts and doughnut holes 1½ minutes on each side, until golden brown. Drain on paper towels. Serve plain, dusted with powdered or granulated sugar, or glazed.

French Market Doughnut Squares

These lemon-flavored doughnuts puff up to resemble little pillows.

1 (¼-ounce) envelope active dry yeast
¼ cup warm water (105° to 115°F.)
⅓ cup granulated sugar
3½ cups all-purpose flour
1 tablespoon baking powder
1 teaspoon salt

¾ teaspoon grated nutmeg
1 cup heavy cream
2 eggs
1 tablespoon grated lemon zest
Oil for frying
Powdered sugar

1. In a 1-cup glass measure, sprinkle the yeast over the warm water. Add a pinch of granulated sugar and stir to mix. Let stand 5 minutes, until foamy. In a medium bowl, combine the flour, baking powder, salt, and nutmeg.

2. In the small bowl of an electric mixer on medium speed, beat the heavy cream, eggs, and remaining granulated sugar until light and fluffy. Pour into a large bowl. Add the dissolved yeast and lemon zest. Stir to mix. Blend in the flour mixture until the dough is soft and easy to handle. Divide the dough in half.

3. On a floured surface, roll out half the dough to a 15 × 5-inch rectangle. Cut lengthwise in half, then crosswise into 2½-inch squares. Repeat with the remaining dough.

4. Pour 1½ inches of oil into a deep fryer. Heat to 365°F. Lifting the doughnuts with a wide slotted metal spatula, lower 2 or 3 at a time into the hot oil. As the doughnuts rise to the surface, turn them over. Fry the doughnuts 1 minute on each side, until puffy and golden brown. Drain on paper towels. Dust with powdered sugar while still warm.

Fried Desserts

When it comes to dessert, even those of you with the strongest willpower will waver and, when looking for that extra-special, on-the-spot dessert, look to the deep fryer. There are an amazing number of desserts from many countries around the world that are deep-fried, and I probably could have done a whole cookbook on them. There are the fun desserts we find at state fairs and street festivals; sugar-dusted Italian Zeppole and Pennsylvania Dutch Funnel Cakes. There are fruit fritters—apple and banana, and fruit empanadas from South America, New Orleans' Calas—sweet fried rice fritters, Greek Loukoumades, small balls of fried dough bathed in a honey syrup, and Chinese Crystal Apples—batter-dipped and fried, coated with a sugar syrup cooked to a candy stage, and dipped into ice water to form a crystal hard coating, and Buñuelos, a light crispy sweet, delicious with Mexican coffee or chocolate.

These and other desserts in the chapter are just as sweet and easy to prepare with the deep fryer.

Hints and Tips

- Read the recipe thoroughly to achieve the best results in both preparation and frying.
- Aerate the flour with a fork before measuring.
- Use large eggs in the recipes.

Sweet Fritter Batter

This all-purpose sweet fritter batter can be used to coat any type of fruit—fresh, dried, or canned—for frying. I've given a couple of my favorites in the recipes that follow.

MAKES 1½ CUPS BATTER, ENOUGH TO COAT 2 POUNDS OF FRUIT

1 cup sifted all-purpose flour

1 tablespoon powdered sugar

1 teaspoon baking powder

¼ teaspoon salt

2 eggs

½ cup milk

1 teaspoon vegetable oil

1 teaspoon grated lemon zest

1. On a sheet of wax paper, combine the flour, powdered sugar, baking powder, and salt. Stir with a fork to mix.

2. In a medium bowl, whisk together the eggs, milk, oil, and lemon zest. Add the flour mixture and whisk until smooth. Use as directed in the following recipes.

Banana Fritters

Use firm, slightly underripe bananas as they will hold their shape better. The bananas will soften when fried in the batter.

MAKES 4 TO 6 SERVINGS

Oil for frying
Sweet Fritter Batter (page 184)
4 large, slightly underripe bananas,
    about 7 inches long

1 tablespoon fresh lemon or lime juice
½ teaspoon grated nutmeg
Powdered sugar, honey, or sweetened
    whipped cream

1. Pour 1 inch of oil into a deep fryer. Heat to 375°F. Meanwhile, prepare the Sweet Fritter Batter.

2. Peel the bananas and slice on a diagonal into 1-inch chunks. Place in a large bowl. Sprinkle with the lemon juice and nutmeg; toss gently to mix.

3. One at a time, dip the banana chunks into the batter, letting the excess drip back into the bowl. Fry 3 or 4 pieces at a time in the hot oil for 3 to 4 minutes, until golden brown, turning once. Drain on paper towels. Serve warm, dusted with powdered sugar, drizzled with warm honey, or topped with a dollop of sweetened whipped cream.

Dutch Apple Fritters

Oil for frying
Sweet Fritter Batter (page 184)
4 large Golden Delicious apples (about
7 ounces each)

1 tablespoon fresh lemon juice
¾ teaspoon apple pie spice
Powdered sugar and vanilla ice cream
(optional)

1. Pour 1 inch of oil into a deep fryer. Heat to 375°F. Meanwhile, prepare the Sweet Fritter Batter.

2. Peel and core the apples and slice crosswise into ½-inch rings. Place in a large bowl. Sprinkle with the lemon juice and the pie spice; toss lightly to coat.

3. Dip the apple rings, a few at a time, into the batter, letting the excess drip back into the bowl. Fry 3 or 4 rings at a time for 3 to 4 minutes, until golden brown, turning once. Drain on paper towels. Serve warm, with a dusting of powdered sugar and ice cream, if desired.

Fried Apple Pies

These miniature fried pies are filled with a thick homemade applesauce.

MAKES 16 PIES

2 cups peeled, cored, and coarsely chopped
   Cortland or other baking apples
¼ cup granulated sugar
1 tablespoon fresh lemon juice
¼ teaspoon apple pie spice or ground
   cinnamon

1 tablespoon cornstarch
Baking Powder Pastry (recipe follows)
Oil for frying
Powdered sugar or Vanilla Glaze (page
   161)

1. In a medium saucepan, combine the chopped apples, sugar, lemon juice, and apple pie spice. Bring to a boil over medium heat. Reduce the heat to low and cook, stirring occasionally, until the apples are soft, about 10 minutes.

2. In a small cup, combine the cornstarch with 1 tablespoon of water. Stir into the apples. Cook and stir until the mixture comes to a boil; boil 1 minute. Place in a small bowl. Let cool. Cover with plastic wrap and refrigerate until cold, about 1 hour.

3. Roll the pastry out on a lightly floured surface with a floured rolling pin to noodle thinness (¹⁄₁₆ inch). Cut the pastry into 4-inch rounds, using a floured cutter (or use the plastic top of a 1-pound coffee can and cut around the top with a small sharp knife). Remove the trimmings from around the pastry rounds. Place the pastry rounds on a baking sheet. Reroll the trimmings to make more rounds.

4. Place 1 level tablespoon of the apple filling in the center of each pastry. Fold the pastry over the filling and pinch to seal. Press down with the floured tines of a fork; turn over and press again.

5. Pour 1 inch of oil into a deep fryer. Heat to 375°F. Fry 3 or 4 pies at a time for 4 minutes, or until golden, turning once. Drain on paper towels. Serve warm or at room temperature, dusted with powdered sugar or drizzled with Vanilla Glaze.

Baking Powder Pastry

2 cups all-purpose flour
1 teaspoon baking powder
¼ teaspoon salt

8 tablespoons (1 stick) unsalted butter,
  cut up
6 tablespoons ice water

In a large bowl, combine the flour, baking powder, and salt. Cut in the butter with a pastry cutter or 2 knives until the mixture resembles cornmeal. Sprinkle the pastry with the ice water. Stir with a fork until moistened. Gather the pastry into a ball.

Zeppole

One of the biggest and most famous street fairs in New York City is the Feast of San Gennaro in Little Italy. A must for the occasion are zeppole—sugar-dusted fried dough balls, which are presented in a brown paper bag.

MAKES 22 TO 24 ZEPPOLE

2 cups all-purpose flour

2 teaspoons baking powder

¼ teaspoon salt

2 eggs

1 teaspoon vanilla extract

⅓ cup granulated sugar

½ cup milk

Oil for frying

Powdered sugar

1. On wax paper, combine the flour, baking powder, and salt. Mix with a fork.

2. In a large bowl, beat the eggs, vanilla, and sugar until well mixed. Stir in the milk. Add the flour mixture and stir to thoroughly combine. The batter will be thick and sticky. Cover the bowl with plastic wrap and let stand at room temperature for 30 minutes.

3. Pour 1½ inches of oil into a deep fryer. Heat to 375°F. Scoop up a tablespoonful of the dough (about the size of a drop cookie) and, using a rubber spatula, slide the dough off the spoon and into the hot fat. Fry 4 or 5 at a time for 3½ to 4 minutes, until golden brown, turning once or twice. Drain on paper towels. Dust with powdered sugar. Serve warm.

Fried Lemon Custard with Lemon Sauce

Several ethnic cuisines have a variation on fried custard, among them Chinese, Middle Eastern, and Mexican. This custard is creamy smooth, surrounded with a crunchy zwieback and almond crust.

MAKES 16 PIECES

Vegetable cooking spray
½ cup cornstarch
½ cup granulated sugar
3 cups milk
1 teaspoon vanilla extract
1 teaspoon grated lemon zest

2 eggs
¾ cup zwieback crumbs (9 rusks)
¾ cup ground blanched almonds
Oil for frying
Lemon Sauce (recipe follows)
Powdered sugar

1. Lightly coat an 8-inch square baking pan with cooking spray.

2. In a medium saucepan, stir together the cornstarch and granulated sugar. Gradually stir in the milk until smooth. Add the vanilla and lemon zest. Cook over medium heat, stirring, until the mixture comes to a boil and thickens, about 12 minutes; boil 1 minute longer. Pour the custard into the prepared pan and spread evenly. Place a piece of plastic wrap directly onto the surface of the custard. Let cool slightly, then refrigerate overnight.

3. In a pie plate, beat the eggs until well blended. In another pie plate, combine the zwieback crumbs with the almonds.

4. Cut the custard into 16 squares. Coat each custard square lightly with the crumbs. Working with 1 custard square at a time, dip into the egg, then back into the crumb mixture, making sure the custard square is completely covered with the crumbs (a fork helps). Place the custard squares on a wire rack set over a baking sheet.

5. Pour 1 inch of oil into a deep fryer. Heat to 375°F. Using a slotted spoon, carefully lower 1 custard square into the hot oil. Fry 3 or 4 squares at a time for 1 minute, or until golden. Lift the custard squares out with the slotted spoon and drain on paper towels. Serve warm, with Lemon Sauce and a dusting of powdered sugar.

Lemon Sauce

MAKES 1¼ CUPS

½ cup sugar
1½ tablespoons cornstarch
1 cup hot water

1 tablespoon butter
1 tablespoon grated lemon zest
1 tablespoon fresh lemon juice

In a small saucepan, combine the sugar with the cornstarch. Gradually stir in the hot water until smooth. Cook over medium heat, stirring, until the mixture comes to a boil and thickens slightly; boil 1 minute. Remove from the heat. Stir in the butter, lemon zest, and lemon juice. Serve warm.

Bueñuelos

These light and crispy Mexican puffs are traditionally served drenched with a thick syrup, but I prefer them as suggested below, with just a dusting of anise-flavored brown sugar.

MAKES 16 TO 17 BUEÑUELOS

2 cups all-purpose flour
2 teaspoons baking powder
1 teaspoon salt
4 tablespoons softened butter
⅓ cup sugar

2 eggs
¼ cup milk
Oil for frying
Anise Sugar (recipe follows)

1. On wax paper, combine the flour, baking powder, and salt. Mix with a fork.

2. In a large bowl, beat the butter and the sugar with an electric mixer on medium speed until crumbly. Beat in the eggs until combined. Blend in the milk. Add 1 cup of the flour mixture, beating just until combined. Stir in the remaining flour mixture with a wooden spoon to make a soft dough.

3. Turn the dough out onto a lightly floured surface. Knead 3 minutes, or until the dough is smooth. Roll out ¼ inch thick with a floured rolling pin. Cut the dough into rounds with a 2¾- to 3-inch cutter. Gather the trimmings to make more bueñuelos. With a rolling pin, roll each round to a thin 4-inch round.

4. Pour 1½ inches of oil into a deep fryer. Heat to 375°F. Lower 2 or 3 bueñuelos at a time into the hot oil and fry 1 minute on each side, or until golden brown. The bueñuelos will puff up like pillows. Drain on paper towels. Serve warm, dusted with Anise Sugar.

Anise Sugar

½ cup firmly packed light brown
   sugar

1 teaspoon anise seed

Place the ingredients in a food processor or blender. Whirl until the anise seeds are crushed slightly. Place in a food storage bag for dusting the bueñuelos.

Loukoumades

A national favorite, these traditional Greek fried dough puffs are dipped in honey and sprinkled with cinnamon. They can also be topped with chopped pistachios, walnuts, or sesame seeds.

MAKES 12 SERVINGS OF ABOUT 6 EACH

1 (¼-ounce) envelope active dry yeast
½ cup very warm water (105° to 115°F.)
2 tablespoons sugar
⅔ cup milk
2 eggs
1 teaspoon salt
⅓ cup sour cream
3½ cups all-purpose flour
Oil for frying
Honey Syrup (recipe follows)
Ground cinnamon and chopped nuts
    or sesame seeds

1. Sprinkle the yeast into the warm water. Add a pinch of sugar and stir to dissolve the yeast. Let stand 5 to 8 minutes until the mixture is foamy and double in volume.
2. In a small saucepan, heat the milk just until bubbles begin to appear at the edge of the pan. Pour the warmed milk into the large bowl of an electric mixer. Add the eggs, remaining sugar, salt, sour cream, and the dissolved yeast. Beat on low speed just until combined. Add 2½ cups of the flour. Beat on medium speed for 3 minutes. Beat in the remaining flour with a wooden spoon to make a soft dough. Cover the bowl with plastic wrap and let rise until double in volume, about 40 to 50 minutes.
3. Pour 1½ inches of oil into a deep fryer. Heat to 365°F.
4. Stir the dough down. Fit a large pastry bag with a large plain tip tube. Place one-third of the dough into the pastry bag. Press enough dough through the tip to form a puff the size of a walnut. Snip off the dough with scissors, letting the dough drop into the hot oil. Fry 5 or 6 at a time for 3 to 4 minutes, until puffed and golden, turning occasionally. Drain on paper towels.

5. For each serving, mound 6 to 7 warm *loukoumades* in a small dessert dish. Drizzle with the Honey Syrup. Dust lightly with cinnamon and sprinkle chopped nuts or sesame seeds on top.

Honey Syrup

This syrup keeps well stored in a covered jar in the refrigerator. It is also good drizzled over pancakes, waffles, French toast, fresh fruit, plain cake, frozen yogurt, or ice cream.

MAKES ABOUT 2 CUPS

1 medium lemon

1 cup sugar

1 cup water

1 (2½-inch) cinnamon stick

1 cup honey

1. Using a zester, strip the peel from the lemon or remove the colored peel with a swivel-bladed vegetable peeler, being careful not to include the white pith. Cut into thin strips. You will need 1 tablespoon. Squeeze 1 tablespoon lemon juice from the lemon.

2. In a medium saucepan, combine the lemon zest, sugar, water, and cinnamon stick. Bring to a boil. Reduce the heat to low and cook without stirring until the mixture is syrupy, about 20 to 25 minutes (230°F. on a candy thermometer). Remove the syrup from the heat.

3. Stir in the honey. Serve warm or at room temperature. If stored in the refrigerator, reheat over low heat, stirring occasionally.

Italian Honey Balls

Called piniollati *in Italy and served during the holiday season, these tiny fried balls are coated with honey syrup, shaped into one impressive mound, and sprinkled with multicolored sprinkles. You can also shape them into serving-size portions. They do take time to prepare, so it's pleasant to turn it into a family project. To make ahead, do not coat with honey. Store for up to a week in a tightly covered container. Before serving, coat with the honey syrup and sprinkles.*

MAKES 2½ POUNDS, 8 TO 10 SERVINGS

4 cups all-purpose flour
½ teaspoon salt
1 tablespoon finely shredded lemon or orange zest, plus 1 tablespoon julienne strips of lemon or orange zest
4 eggs
½ cup solid vegetable shortening

¾ cup plus 1 tablespoon sugar
Solid vegetable shortening or oil for frying
½ cup honey
2 tablespoons pine nuts (pignoli)
Multicolored candy sprinkles, for garnish

1. In a large bowl, combine the flour, salt, and lemon or orange zest. Mix with a fork. Make a well in the center. Add the eggs and stir to combine.
2. In a small saucepan, melt the shortening with ¾ cup of the sugar and ¼ cup water over low heat. Stir into the flour mixture until the mixture cleans the sides of the bowl. The dough will be sticky.
3. Turn the dough out onto a lightly floured surface. Knead 3 to 4 minutes, until the dough is shiny and smooth and no longer sticks to the surface. Shape into a ball. Cover with the bowl and let rest 15 minutes.
4. Cut small pieces from the dough and roll into ropes ½ inch in diameter on an unfloured surface. With a sharp knife, cut into ¼-inch pieces. Set the little pieces of

dough aside on large baking sheets. They will stick together but will separate during frying. Keep the dough covered to prevent drying out.

5. Place the shortening in small pieces in a deep fryer and melt following the manufacturer's directions or pour in 1½ inches of oil. Heat to 375°F.

6. Fry a handful of the little dough pieces at a time in the hot oil until golden brown, about 2 to 2½ minutes. Tap them with a wooden spoon to separate if they stick together during frying. Remove with the fryer basket or a slotted spoon. Drain on paper towels. Repeat with the remaining dough pieces.

7. In a large deep saucepan, combine the honey, remaining 1 tablespoon sugar, and 1 tablespoon water. Heat over low heat, stirring occasionally, until the honey begins to bubble. Add the julienne lemon or orange zest and the fried balls; toss to coat. Cook, stirring, until the honey coats the balls, about 5 minute. Stir in the pine nuts. Turn out onto a jelly-roll pan. Let cool. When cool enough to handle, shape into a single mound, or into 8 to 10 separate mounds. Sprinkle with candy sprinkles. Store at room temperature, lightly covered with foil.

Pineapple-Orange Empanadas

These fried turnovers are of Mexican origin, but versions can also be found in Cuba and South America. Empanadas can be large or appetizer size, savory or sweet. With these dessert pies, I allow two or three per person.

MAKES 16 EMPANADAS, 8 SERVINGS

1 (8-ounce) can crushed pineapple
with its juices, undrained
2 tablespoons granulated sugar
1 tablespoon cornstarch
2 teaspoons butter
1 teaspoon grated orange or lemon
zest

Empanada Pastry (recipe follows)
Solid vegetable shortening or oil for
frying
Powdered sugar

1. In a medium saucepan, combine the crushed pineapple with its juices, granulated sugar, cornstarch, butter, and orange or lemon zest. Cook over medium heat, stirring, until the mixture is bubbly and thick, about 2 minutes. Remove from the heat and let cool to room temperature.

2. Turn the empanada pastry dough out onto a lightly floured work surface. Knead 6 to 8 times until smooth. Roll out the dough 1/16 inch thick (noodle thickness). Cut out rounds with a 4-inch floured cutter, or use the plastic top of a 1-pound coffee can and cut around the top with the point of a small knife. Lift the excess dough off and set the pastry rounds aside. Reroll the trimmings as often as necessary until you have 16 rounds.

3. Fill each pastry round with a scant tablespoon of the pineapple filling. Working with 1 at a time, moisten the edge of the pastry round lightly with water. Fold in half over the filling to form a half moon. Press the edges together. Press the edges again with a floured fork on both sides to seal.

4. Place the shortening in small pieces in a deep fryer and melt, following the manufacturer's directions, or pour in 1½ inches of oil. Heat to 375°F. Carefully slide 4 or 5 empanadas at a time into the hot oil. Fry 2 minutes on each side, until golden. Drain on paper towels. Serve warm or at room temperature, dusted with powdered sugar.

Empanada Pastry

MAKES ENOUGH PASTRY FOR 16 EMPANADAS

1½ cups all-purpose flour
1 teaspoon baking powder
¼ teaspoon salt

⅓ cup solid vegetable shortening
⅓ cup milk

In a large bowl, combine the flour, baking powder, and salt. Mix with a fork. Cut in the shortening with a pastry blender or 2 knives until the mixture resembles cornmeal. Sprinkle on the milk. Mix the pastry with a fork until the dough starts to cling together. If necessary, add 1 teaspoon more milk. The pastry should not be wet or sticky. With the palm of your hand, knead the dough in the bowl until the mixture comes together.

Pumpkin Empanadas

Pumpkin spiked with pumpkin pie spice flavors these empanadas. You can also serve them as a vegetable side dish without the cinnamon sugar topping or as a hot appetizer with mulled cider for Thanksgiving.

MAKES 16 EMPANADAS

1 cup canned solid-pack pumpkin (not pumpkin pie filling)
⅓ cup firmly packed light brown sugar
1 teaspoon pumpkin pie spice

Empanada Pastry (page 199)
Solid vegetable shortening or vegetable oil for frying
Cinnamon Sugar (page 172)

1. In a medium bowl, place the pumpkin, brown sugar, and pumpkin pie spice. Blend well.

2. Turn the empanada pastry out onto a lightly floured work surface. Knead 6 to 8 times until smooth. Roll out the dough ¹⁄₁₆ inch thick (noodle thickness). Cut out rounds with a 4-inch floured cutter, or use the plastic top from a 1-pound coffee can and cut around the top with the point of a sharp knife. Lift the excess dough off and set the rounds aside. Roll out the trimmings as often as necessary until you have 16 rounds.

3. Fill each round with 1 level tablespoon of the pumpkin filling. Working with 1 pastry round at a time, moisten the edges lightly with water. Fold in half over the filling to form a half moon. Press the edges together. Press the edges again with a floured fork on both sides to seal.

4. Place the shortening in small pieces in a deep fryer and melt, following the manufacturer's directions, or pour in 1½ inches of oil. Heat to 375°F. Carefully slide 4 or 5 empanadas at a time into the hot fat. Fry 2 minutes on each side, until golden. Drain on paper towels. Serve plain or sprinkle with Cinnamon Sugar while slightly warm.

Fried Bow Ties

These fried noodle-like cookies are flavored with lemon and vanilla. They are best eaten the same day they are made.

MAKES 2 DOZEN BOW TIES

¼ cup buttermilk
2 egg yolks
2 tablespoons vegetable oil
1 tablespoon granulated sugar
1½ teaspoons grated lemon zest
1 teaspoon vanilla extract

¼ teaspoon salt
1 cup plus 2 tablespoons all-purpose
    flour
Oil for frying
Powdered sugar

1. In a medium bowl, whisk together the buttermilk, egg yolks, vegetable oil, granulated sugar, lemon zest, vanilla, and salt. Stir in ¾ cup of the flour.

2. Place the remaining flour on a work surface. Turn the dough out onto the flour and knead in enough flour so the dough is easy to handle. Roll out to a 12-inch square.

3. Cut the dough into 4 × 1½-inch strips. Make a 1-inch slit down the center of each strip with a small knife. Pull 1 end of the dough through the slit to make a bowtie shape with a single loop.

4. Pour 1 inch of oil into a deep fryer. Heat to 365°F. Fry the bow ties, a few at a time, for 1½ to 2 minutes, until golden, turning once. Remove with a slotted spoon. Drain on paper towels. Sift with powdered sugar while slightly warm. Serve at once.

Calas

Creole women vendors in New Orleans would stroll down the streets of the French Quarter, wooden bowls perched on their heads, shouting the lyrical cry of, "Bel Calas, tout chauds" (Lovely rice, piping hot.). Since these fritters must be started the night before, they are a perfect addition to a Sunday brunch. Serve with a variety of toppings: warmed honey or maple syrup, raspberry or strawberry jam, and, of course, a chicory-flavored coffee.

MAKES 28 CALAS

2 cups cold water
1 tablespoon butter
½ teaspoon salt
½ cup long-grain white rice
1 (¼-ounce) envelope active dry yeast
½ cup warm water (105° to 115°F.)
3 tablespoons sugar, plus a pinch
  more for dusting

3 eggs, slightly beaten
1 cup all-purpose flour
¼ teaspoon ground cinnamon
¼ teaspoon grated nutmeg
¼ teaspoon vanilla extract
Oil for frying

1. In a medium saucepan, bring the cold water, butter, and salt to a boil over high heat. Add the rice and stir once. Reduce the heat, cover, and simmer 25 minutes, or until the rice is very soft. Drain off any excess water. Place the rice in a large bowl and mash with a potato masher or a wooden spoon. Let cool to lukewarm.

2. In a 1-cup glass measure, sprinkle the yeast over the warm water. Add a pinch of sugar and stir to dissolve the yeast. Let stand 5 minutes until the mixture is bubbly. Stir into the cooled mashed rice. Cover with plastic wrap and let stand in a warm spot away from drafts overnight.

3. The next day, add 3 tablespoons sugar, the eggs, flour, cinnamon, nutmeg, and vanilla to the rice mixture. Beat well. Cover and let rise away from drafts for 30 minutes. The mixture will start to get bubbles on the surface.

4. Pour 1½ inches of oil into a deep fryer. Heat to 375°F. Scoop up the dough by heaping tablespoons and, using a rubber spatula to dislodge it, carefully slide into the hot oil. Fry 3 or 4 at a time for 2 to 3 minutes, until golden, turning once. Drain on paper towels. Sprinkle with sugar and serve while still warm.

Fried Ricotta Puffs

This delicate, light Italian fritter would go well with a cup of espresso or cappuccino.

MAKES 16 RICOTTA PUFFS

½ cup all-purpose flour

1 teaspoon baking powder

¼ teaspoon salt

2 eggs

2 tablespoons granulated sugar

1 cup whole-milk ricotta cheese

1½ teaspoons vanilla extract

Oil for frying

Powdered sugar

1. On wax paper, combine the flour, baking powder, and salt. Mix with a fork.

2. In a large bowl, whisk together the eggs, granulated sugar, ricotta, and vanilla until creamy smooth. Stir in the flour mixture; the batter will be somewhat thin.

3. Pour 1½ inches of oil into a deep fryer. Heat to 375°F. Carefully drop the batter by level tablespoons into the hot oil, using a small rubber spatula to help slide it off the spoon. Fry 5 to 6 at a time, turning occasionally, until golden brown, about 2 minutes. Drain on paper towels. Dust with powdered sugar and serve while still warm.

Funnel Cakes

From Pennsylvania Dutch country, these delicate spiral fried dessert breads are a favorite at street carnivals and state fairs. A special pitcher with a spout at one end is usually used, but a traditional funnel with a ½-inch interior diameter works for the home cook. These cakes are usually dusted with powdered sugar, but they're also good topped with molasses or maple syrup. Do not use the fryer basket when making these cakes, as the batter will stick to it. It really takes two sets of hands to make this easily: one to hold the funnel and the other to spoon in the batter.

MAKES 8 TO 10 FUNNEL CAKES

2 cups all-purpose flour
1 teaspoon baking powder
½ teaspoon salt
2 eggs
1½ cups milk

½ teaspoon vanilla extract
Oil for frying
Powdered sugar, molasses, or maple
    syrup

1. On wax paper, combine the flour, baking powder, and salt. Mix with a fork.

2. In a medium bowl, whisk together the eggs, milk, and vanilla. Whisk in the flour mixture until the batter is creamy yellow and smooth.

3. Pour 1 inch of oil into a deep fryer. Heat to 360°F. Holding a funnel with a ½-inch inside diameter and using a finger to plug the bottom, pour ⅓ cup batter into the funnel. Holding the funnel over the oil, remove your finger and release the batter into the hot oil in a circular motion, working out from the center in a spiral (do not use the wire basket).

4. Fry 2½ minutes, until the bottom of the funnel cake is golden brown. Using 2 wide metal spatulas, carefully turn the cake over. Fry 1 minute longer, or until golden brown on the second side. Lift out between metal spatulas and place on paper towels. Remove any loose pieces of fried batter from the oil. Repeat with the remaining batter. Dust with powdered sugar or drizzle with molasses or maple syrup. Serve warm.

Chinese Crystal Apples

I can never resist this crackly crisp dessert when I see it on a menu in a Chinese restaurant. The preliminary frying of the apples can be done ahead of time, but the final syrup coating and dipping into ice water to make them hard must take place just before serving. To clean the saucepan, fill with cold water and heat over low heat to dissolve the remaining sugar.

MAKES 4 TO 6 SERVINGS

½ cup all-purpose flour
2 tablespoons cornstarch
½ teaspoon baking powder
4 medium Empire, Golden Delicious,
   or other cooking apples

Oil for frying
1⅓ cups sugar
2 tablespoons vegetable oil
1 tablespoon black sesame seeds* or
   toasted regular sesame seeds

1. In a medium bowl, combine the flour, cornstarch, and baking powder. Whisk in ½ cup of water until the batter is thick and smooth. If it seems too thick, add 1 to 3 teaspoons more water to make a thick but not runny batter.

2. Peel, halve, and core the apples. Cut each half into 3 equal wedges and pat dry with paper towels.

3. Pour 1½ inches of oil into a deep fryer. Heat to 365°F. Drop the apple wedges into the batter and turn to coat well. Lift out 1 at a time with tongs, letting the excess batter drip back into the bowl. Fry 3 or 4 at a time until pale gold, about 1½ to 2 minutes. Transfer to a rack set over a baking sheet.

*Available in Asian markets and in the spice section of some supermarkets.

4. Fill a large bowl with ice and water. Lightly butter a large serving platter. In a medium saucepan, combine the sugar, ⅔ cup of water, and the 2 tablespoons vegetable oil. Bring to a boil over medium heat, stirring to dissolve the sugar. Cook at a low boil without stirring until the syrup reaches the hard-crack stage (310° to 320°F. on a candy thermometer), begins to thicken, and turns light brown at the edges. Immediately remove from the heat. Stir in the black sesame seeds.

5. Working quickly, drop the apples, a few at a time, into the hot syrup. Turn to coat with a fork. Lift the apples out and immediately drop into the bowl of ice and water. Lift the apples out of the ice water with a slotted spoon. Place on the buttered platter. Serve at once.

Index

209

Crispy red onion shreds, 130
Croquettes
  ham, with cheese sauce, 84
  potato, with goat cheese and scallions, 129
  suppli al telefono, 136
Crullers
  churros, 173
  orange, 164
Crumb coatings, 92–93
Crystal apples, Chinese, 206
Cumin-flavored cornmeal chips, 147
Curried yogurt sauce, lamb meatballs in, 90
Custard with lemon sauce, fried lemon, 190

Deep fryers, 1, 3–4
  choosing, 3
  cleanup, 4
  makes and models, 5–9
  oil temperature, 4
  safety, 4–5
Delonghi Cool Touch Roto Deep Fryer, 6–7
Desserts, fried, 183–207. *See also* Empanadas; Fritters
  apple pies, fried, 187
  bow ties, fried, 201
  buñuelos, 192
  calas, 202
  crystal apples, Chinese, 206
  funnel cakes, 205
  honey balls, Italian, 196
  lemon custard with lemon sauce, fried, 190
  loukoumades, 194
  zeppole, 189
Dip(s). *See also* Salsa
  blue cheese, 15
  cilantro cream, 32
  honey mustard, 48
Double-crust sausage pizzas, 76
Double-dipped fried chicken, 42
Doughnut(s), 158–82
  banana spice, 167
  cake, 160
  carrot cake, 178
  chocolate-sour cream, 168
  hints and tips, 159
  jelly, 174
  lemon buttermilk, 162
  old-fashioned cinnamon, 171
  potato, 181
  spiced pumpkin, 176
  squares, French Market, 182

walnut puffs, 177
zucchini cake, 180
Drumsticks, garlic-fried, 51
Dutch apple fritters, 186

Egg rolls, vegetable, 36
Eggs, Scotch, 78
Empanada(s)
  pastry, 199
  pineapple-orange, 198
  pumpkin, 200
Equipment, 11

Falafel with lemon tahini sauce, 120
Fish, 92–116. *See also* Shellfish
  catfish with rémoulade sauce, fried, 96
  and chips, 104
  codfish cakes, salt, 102
  fingers with garlic sauce, 106
  flounder, goujonette of, 101
  fry, mixed, 98
  hints and tips, 93
  in tempura, 114
Flounder, goujonette of, 101
Fontina sticks, walnut-crusted, 18
Frankfurters
  in corn dawgs, 70
  in pigs in a poke, 33
French-fried okra, 123
French-fried sweet potato sticks, 124
French fries, 125
French Market doughnut squares, 182
Fresh tomato salsa, 80
Fried apple pies, 187
Fried bow ties, 201
Fried calamari, 94
Fried catfish with rémoulade sauce, 96
Fried clams, 113
Fried green tomatoes with aioli and pancetta, 126
Fried lemon custard with lemon sauce, 190
Fried onion rings, 131
Fried oysters, 111
Fried parsley, 135
Fried potato skins with Cheddar cheese and bacon, 23
Fried ricotta puffs, 204
Fried soft-shell crabs with lemon-basil butter, 108
Fried whole artichokes, 132
Fried zucchini strips, 134
Fritter(s)
  banana, 185